# AS I TRACE AGAIN
# THY WINDING HILL

# AS I TRACE AGAIN THY WINDING HILL

## HARROW ON THE HILL

A Tapestry of
Prose and Verse

Dorothy Boux ❦ Eliane Wilson

SHEPHEARD ~ WALWYN

First published 1981 by
Shepheard-Walwyn (Publishers) Ltd
12/13 Henrietta Street
London WC2E 8LH


ISBN 0 85683 053 4




Printed in Great Britain
on Harrow Book Wove
by Robert HARTNOLL, Ltd. Bodmin, Cornwall

To the memory of
MAURICE RENTZNIK
my father
Eliane Wilson

Bright stars of youth that through my orbit spring,
Kaleidoscopic images of light
Undimmed by skews and double, a delight
Of mind and being,
Illuminating that which is;
Textured shadows cast and tapestried together.

Perpetual patterns – bell and bill,
Prep., and the pull of duty on desire,
But subtler still –
'I want . . . I need. . . I do not know. . .
Direction. . .? Why am I here. . .?'

I listen to your hearts, to see and know
Through you, the common thread.
Common? Uncommon, that fine thread
That binds you to each other,
To long history upon a hill,
To fabric ever present,
To a destiny unknown as yet,
But weft on time.

So, mirror to your light –
Fond inspiration –
I take my pen, and write . . .

THE CALLIGRAPHER

# ACKNOWLEDGEMENTS

We are deeply indebted to the Governors of Harrow School who have allowed us to research in the archives of the School and for their permission to quote and reproduce from them extensively; also to the Head Master of Harrow, Mr. Michael Hoban, for his kind interest in the book.

We are grateful to His Honour Judge Verney who wrote the Foreword.

To Sir Arthur Bryant, who has kindly allowed us to use quotations from his books and to Sir John Betjeman for allowing us to reproduce his poem "Harrow on the Hill", we would like to express our gratitude.

We are particularly grateful to Mr. Ronald Watkins, Mr. James Morwood and Mr. Michael Rees for their essays on Shakespeare, Sheridan and Byron which were especially written for this book.

For permission to reproduce poems and prose from copyrighted books, our thanks are due to the following:

John Murray (Publishers) Limited for a quotation from "The Hill" by Horace Annesley Vachell.
Oxford University Press for poems from "Trophy for an Unknown Soldier" by R.W. Moore (1952)
Arthur Stockwell Limited for "The Second Eleven" by H. Cracroft White. We also thank the proprietors of Punch for permission to print "Private and Confidential".

We thank several masters at Harrow School for their encouragement and help during the preparation and editing of the book, especially Mr. C.H. Shaw.

We also thank Mrs. Melisa Treasure for her proofreading of the manuscript, her comments and corrections; Mrs. Hedi Southwell for help with calligraphic corrections and index, and James Elliott for assisting with the preparation of illustrations; finally our husbands.

If by inadvertance, copyright material has been included in these pages without permission or if we have failed to trace the publisher we hope that our sincere apologies will be accepted.

# TABLE OF CONTENTS

# FOREWORD

It is difficult to explain the devotion which the Hill inspires, but there is no denying that devotion. The feeling has been shared by many and is life-long. It is not sentimental in the mawkish sense but is based on emotion, and each devotee will have his own thoughts about it.

Perhaps the starting-point is the site which John Lyon found for his School, on a hill but not dominating that hill. The School's buildings have expanded widely from Lyon's original one, but the commanding feature of Harrow remains that which he saw ~ St. Mary's Church. "The Hill's grey spire still greets the day" and reminds us of the words of the 121st Psalm.

The genius of a school is not derived merely from its site and buildings. It must depend very largely on those who work there. It is often overlooked how much is due to those who devote their energies to teaching and thereby inspire and encourage the young. Harrow has been fortunate in attracting and retaining many outstanding members of staff; and in the context of this book it is right to recall that the Songs (both words and music) are almost entirely due to Masters.

"None so narrow the range of Harrow, welcome poet and statesman too". Thanks to those teachers as well as to innate abilities, the boys who have gone from the School into "the wider life to be" have taken with them many and various talents which they have used and have wanted to use in the service of mankind, but the extent of that service is wider far than the two categories of "doer and dreamer" and is only partly to be understood from what they have written and what they are recorded as having done.

Buildings, masters, boys are all represented here in this beautiful book, which is a collection of illustrations of our Hill in word and picture that will renew for some and awaken in others the realization of what Harrow means. There is every reason to be deeply grateful to Eliane Wilson for the selection and creation she has so lovingly made; to Dorothy Boux for the exquisite calligraphy which embellishes it; and to them both for a volume worthy of its subject.

Having an unbroken family link with Harrow, which has continued for over 200 years, I am prejudiced; but I am thrilled to find and delighted to commend this tribute to the place I love and this expression of its ethos.

LAWRENCE. J. VERNEY

# PREFACE

" I had long loved Harrow and knew that the Hill was holy ground, ghost ~ haunted from the history ~ making hours of the far ~ off years.

I had wondered how it might be possible to reveal to Harrow, in a way to be understanded of the people, that the very dust we trod upon was mystical and mighty ~ and I thought of a pageant..."

So wrote Sydney Walton, chairman of the Harrow Historical Pageant which took place on the Hill from June 28th to July 5th in 1923, and for which Frank Lascelles, Master of the Pageant, marshalled more than three thousand performers.

On the first day, four Knights ~ at ~ Arms rode from Harrow to Wesminster, bearing a sealed message which they delivered to the Prime Minister, Stanley Baldwin, at number ten, Downing Street : ~

## TO THE PRIME MINISTER OF ENGLAND,

Greetings are borne by this message of good will brought from Harrow on the Hill to Downing Street by riders who each evening are taking part in the Historical Pageant, wherein the long centuries of adventure and triumph which hallow the Ancient Parish are made to live again in their colour and wonder.

Great and severe are the anxious problems which in these present days oppress the mind of the Prime Minister of England and to cheer and encourage him in his task for the people's weal is this greeting sent with affection and glorifying it is the fragrance of the Hill.

In the speech which in the Pageant Queen Elizabeth doth make are the words following :—

'There shall issue from the portals of thy School Statesmen grave as Burleigh, Prelates wise as Parker, Poets sweet as Sidney, Captains gallant as Raleigh, Wits supple as Hatton, and Courtiers dear as Robin Leicester. And all shall serve our common land.'

So do the thousands of performers in the stately Pageant each evening emphasize anew and cherish afresh the memories and traditions and inspirations which in the Parish and around the

Hill are kept in love.
And the Prime Minister of England is in a great
succession and hath a goodly heritage.

HARROW ON THE HILL

This book is our poem of love for the
Hill, verses woven upon the landscape
of ancient and modern history, the
history of the Hill.
　　May the reader now wander
　　　　through the Hill
　　　　　with us . . .

# The hill

Upraised before recorded history
The lofty summit of this ageless hill
Has been a vantage point for centuries;
For saxons, kings - and we who walk here still.
Its verdant shoulders graciously have borne
Old Lanfranc's church and splendid Harrow school;
Its winding streets and canting road well worn
By journeyings both grand and minuscule.
How many boys reached manhood on its back
Gazing out worldwards from its gentle height?
What deeds they did, for none did courage lack,
These sons of Harrow in their glory's flight!
Beneath the public school and churchyard stones,
The Hill stands firm and great renown enthrones.

KENNETH VERITY
1980

1

# THE COMING OF THE GUMENINGS

## APPROXIMATE DATE A.D. 550

The first mention of Harrow in any extant document is the grant of certain lands near 'the Harrow of the Gumenings' by King Offa to Abbot Stidberht in AD 767.

(GUMEN and his tribesmen are seen advancing from the N.E. in the direction of Harrow. At a sign from their chief, they halt and he addresses them.)

Here let us rest, and tarry for a while,
Till Brighthelm, with the band I sent to search
The folds and crests of yonder wooded hill
Return and bring their tidings.
Never yet, since in our ships we left our northern home,
The narrow wick beside the sullen sea,
The sandy hummocks by the long, low shore,
Backed by the shadow of the long, low weald —
Never have I beheld so fair a spot as this.

2

These meadows laughing in the light
This little burn that sparkles as it runs,
These forest slopes that close the northern dale
And yonder hill that god-like fronts the west —
All seem to breathe a welcome. Thank the Gods
Who brought us to this haven out of storm

    (At this moment BRIGHTHELM arrives with
      his band and addresses GUMEN.)

We climbed the ridge, O Gumen, pressing on
Through copse and tangled brushwood to the crest,
There found some scattered huts, untenanted,
And smouldering ruins of an ancient shrine,
Thereby a well of water, clear and sweet,
A level space, steep-fronted to the West,
Whence, like a sea before us, stretched a plain
With marsh and heath and holt, and, here and
                                  there
A wasted croft. But crowning all there stands
A grove of ancient trees, whose mystic shade
It seemed us, were fit dwelling for our Gods.

    (The PRIEST OF WODEN steps forward and
      solemnly addresses the Assembly.)

When first we stept, from out the darksome
                                  weald,
Into the freedom of the sunlit field,
And lingered for a while with dazzled eyes,
I saw a lark from its low nest arise

I marked his flight as heavenward he soared
And such a glad and mastering song outpoured
As seemed to cleave the drifting clouds and thrill
The doubting heart and wake the slumbering will.
The Gods are with us. Here let us uplift
Our thankful hearts and vow our noblest gift.
Yonder shall stand, until the end of things,
Our shrine ~ our Harrow ~ of the Gumenings.

(He pauses and continues with rapt expression)
Mine eyes are dim with age, yet can I see,
Across the mist of years, the days to be.
Voices unknown I hear, and tramp of feet,
The rush of wheels and tumult of the street.
Here upon hill and plain and winding slope,
A world of men shall wake to work and hope;
Here youth shall throng, where knowledge sheds
                                        her ray
And learn to rule by learning to obey.
Here shall a newer line of warriors rise,
In battle fearless and in council wise;
Statesmen who seek no meed of pelf or praise
But to be strong and just, to guide and raise;
Thinkers, who fain would know and searching
                                        find
New powers, new wonders to enrich mankind;
And bards, whose song, the fairest fruit of Time,
Shall lift the souls of men to heights sublime.

4

(GUMEN now steps forward and addresses the assembled tribesmen)

And now to right and ancient custom true
I ask you Kinsmen, Freemen of this folk,
Is this your will – to cease from wandering
And here abide for aye?
TRIBESMEN – Yea! Gumen, yea!

(They spring to their feet and clash their weapons upon their shields in sign of assent)

GUMEN – So be it, then!

LOUIS MORIARTY
(Harrow Historical Pageant – 1923)

# THE FOUNDING OF ST. MARY'S CHURCH

ow in the year of the Incarnation of our Lord 825, a Synodical Council was assembled together from various parts of the Saxon Land at a notable place called Clovesho. And of this venerable Council the President was Wulfred the Archbishop. He summoned the Abbess Cwoenthryth, daughter and heiress of Cenulf, King of Mercia...and the Synod decreed with one accord that she should render to the Archbishop all that her father had by violence taken from him.

THE REVEREND W. DONE-BUSHELL

As an act of reparation, the Abbess surrendered also her lands of Harrow and thus was initiated the long connection between Harrow and the See of Canterbury.

In AD 1087 Archbishop LANFRANC laid the foundation stone of Harrow Church. It was consecrated by his successor ANSELM in AD 1094.

---

EADMER who was a monk at Canterbury when he first met Saint Anselm in the year 1079, and who was to become his friend and inseparable companion, has recalled the consecration – VITA S. ANSELMI – and how the Bishop of London, objecting to the Archbishop of Canterbury performing the dedication, sent an emissary to steal the consecrated oil ...

---

ST. ANSELM was placed by Dante among the great figures of his "Paradiso".

(Canto XII, verso 137)

---

# HOW THE CHRISMATORY WAS STOLEN AT THE DEDICATION OF THE CHURCH AT HARROW, AND HOW IT WAS RESTORED

ANSELM went to his village at Harrow and dedicated the church belonging to his diocese. His predecessor Lanfranc had built it, but had died before he was able to dedicate it.

Among those who came from London for the dedication was a certain cleric who, having thrust himself in among the Archbishop's clerks as if to help them, secretly seized the episcopal chrismatory and made off into the crowd. However, while he was going along the road to London with his stolen property, he turned back, thinking that he had been going in the wrong direction.

But when he came back and found the crowd of people who had come together he realised that he had turned from the right road and so he retraced his steps along the way that he had come.

He went some distance and again it seemed to him that he was going back to the place from which he was running away. This happened several times and he wandered and strayed here and there, not knowing where he was going, so that the people who saw him behaving like this wondered what was the matter with him.

Meanwhile the Archbishop's servants had found that the chrismatory was missing and were rushing about in confusion looking everywhere for the lost vessel, having no idea whom to ask and where to look for it. A rumour of the loss spread among the crowd and the suspicion of many fell on the wandering clerk. He was seized and the stolen vessel was found under his cloak.

The whole affair was reported to the Archbishop, but he, with a mild look and tranquil spirit, at once ordered the fault to be forgiven and the clerk was set free to go to his own home. As soon as he was free, he went off without hesitation along the road which he had been quite unable to keep to when burdened with his theft.

EADMER

In the year of grace AD 1143, Thomas BECKET joined the Household of Theobald, Archbishop of Canterbury, who was holding court at Harrow.
In that court, centre of all the culture and talent of the realm, Becket was soon to become the right hand of Theobald. He rapidly rose to fame and honour and was made Chancellor by the King.

Twenty years later, in the year AD 1163, he returned to the Hill as Thomas the Archbishop.

His third visit to the Hill was in that fateful December 1170. Becket spent three days at the Manor House before leaving for Canterbury to go to his martyrdom.

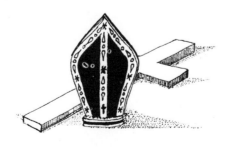

1ST. VILLAGER ~ *We wait for the Lord Abbot of St. Albans. He is gone to Woodstock, at the bidding of Thomas, our Archbishop, and Lord of this Manor of Harrow, to try and win back for him the favour of the young King who holds his court there.*

STRANGER ~ *And so Thomas is with you! I knew it not. Is this his first visit to your Hill?*

1ST. VILLAGER ~ *Nay, nay, we know him well at Harrow. Many of us can remember when he first came hither. It was nigh on thirty years ago. He came to join the household of good Archbishop Theobald ~ Heaven rest his soul! A proper man was Thomas, Gilbert Becket's son, the Portreeve. 'Thomas of London' they called him then, for he was born and bred in Cheapside. Tall and goodly of countenance he was, and nobly clad, fond of his hawk and his hound, and ready with sword and lance.*

2ND. VILLAGER (interrupting) ~ *There stands old Mistress Rose, his hostess, the first night he was ever here.* (Turning to a woman nearby) *Tell us of thy dream, good Mistress.*

HOSTESS ~ Ay, ay! I mind it well. He rode up to the Manor House to see the good Theobald! but he slept with us at the village inn. That night I dreamt I saw him, sitting upon the roof of our church, and his robes hung down and covered the whole church. And ye see my dream came true, for the King made him Archbishop, and head of this church, and of the whole Church of England.

LOUIS MORIARTY.
(in collaboration with Bishop WELLDON)
Harrow Historical Pageant ~ 1923

# HARROVIANA

Hallowed pile our fathers raised,
Ancient fane where God is praised,
Resting place of saints of old,
Refuge of the living fold,
Oh may ages yet to come
Worship in this sacred home!

Crown of all the neighbouring lands,
High and lifted up it stands;
Unto Heaven its lofty finger
Raised, forbids us here to linger;
Calling with its silent voice,
"Heaven or Hell awaits thy choice."

EDWARD SCOTT

15

Over the centuries weddings have regularly
taken place at the church. Richard Harris Barham
(1788 ~ 1845), author of the "Ingoldsby Legends"
and canon at St. Paul's Cathedral had come
to Harrow to do some brass rubbing, but,
finding that the officiating minister was missing,
he married a waiting couple and left this note
for him.

Mr. Bruce, Mr. Bruce,
When the matrimonial noose
You ought here at Harrow to be tying,
If you choose to ride away
As you know you did today,
No wonder bride and bridegroom should
          be crying.

It's a very great abuse
Mr. Bruce, Mr. Bruce,
And you're quite without excuse,
And of very little use
As a curate,
Mr. Bruce.

# LINES WRITTEN BENEATH AN ELM IN THE CHURCHYARD AT HARROW

Spot of my youth! whose hoary branches sigh,
Swept by the breeze that fans thy cloudless sky,
Where now alone I muse, who oft have trod,
With those I lov'd, thy soft and verdant sod;
With those, who scatter'd far, perchance, deplore,
Like me the happy scenes they knew before;
Oh! as I trace again thy winding hill,
Mine eyes admire, my heart adores thee still,
Thou drooping Elm! beneath whose boughs I lay,
And frequent mus'd the twilight hours away;
Where, as they once were wont, my limbs recline,
But, ah! without the thoughts, which, then, were mine;
How do thy branches, moaning to the blast,

Invite the bosom to recall the past,
And seem to whisper, as they gently swell,
"Take, while thou canst, a ling'ring, last farewell!"

When Fate shall chill at length this fever'd breast
And calm its cares and passions into rest,
Oft, have I thought, 'twould soothe my dying hour,
If aught may soothe, when Life resigns her power;
To know, some humbler grave, some narrow cell,
Would hide my bosom, where it lov'd to dwell;
With this fond dream, methinks 'twere sweet to die,
And here it linger'd, here my heart might lie
Here might I sleep, where all my hopes arose,
Scene of my youth, and couch of my repose;
For ever stretch'd beneath this mantling shade,
Prest by the turf, where once my childhood play'd;
Wrapt by the soil that veils the spot I lov'd,
Mix'd with the earth, o'er which my footsteps mov'd
Blest by the tongues that charmed my youthful ear
Mourn'd by the few my soul acknowledg'd here;
Deplor'd by those in early days allied,
And unremember'd by the world beside.

LORD BYRON
(Hours of Idleness ~ 1807)

# BYRON AND ALLEGRA

*I*n 1807 Lord Byron visited Harrow, which he had left with regret in 1805 to go up to Cambridge, and penned the preceding nostalgic lines, dated September 2nd. Years later, exiled at Pisa, Byron recalled Harrow churchyard when bereavement came. His wife had left him in January 1816: he was to see neither her nor their daughter Ada again. Increasingly he set his hopes upon his natural daughter Allegra, fathered before he left England in April 1816.

Allegra was born in Bath on January 12th, 1817. Her mother, Claire Clairmont, brought her to Italy in 1818 with Shelley and his wife Mary, Claire's stepsister. Byron undertook Allegra's upbringing, placing her in a convent school at Bagnacavallo, near Ravenna. Here Shelley was struck by "the beauty of her deep blue eyes", her "contemplative seriousness" yet "excessive vitality". But on April 20th, 1822, Allegra died of a fever. The sorrowing nuns recorded "her rare talents and the lovableness of her character". Byron was heartbroken, and sent her embalmed remains to England for interment at Harrow, "where I once hoped to have laid my own". On September 10th she was buried near the church door by Henry Drury, son of Byron's old Master; but the then Vicar would not allow any memorial to be erected.

All but two years from Allegra's death Byron "lay, Dying for freedom, far away" in Greece: it was April 19th, 1824. On April 19th, 1980, the Byron Society dedicated a memorial to his daughter on the outer porch of Harrow Church.                    MICHAEL REES

19

Beneath these green trees, rising to the skies,
The planter of them, Isaac Greentree lies;
A time shall come when all green trees shall fall,
And Isaac Greentree rise above them all.

Isaac Greentree was a churchwarden in 1696 and the original of the wood panel was dated 1702, but Percy Thornton the historian wrote in 1885 that 'there was a certain family called Greentree who kept what in modern parlance is known as a tuckshop where Byron was wont to regale. When Mr. Greentree died, the poet, in response to the widows desire, wrote an epitaph that was placed on Isaac Greentree's grave'...

We leave it to the reader to decide...

To the Memory
of
WILLIAM    FELIX    LAMBERT

Fourth son of
Charles Lambert Esq.,
of Fitzroy Square, London
who died on the 21st November, 1825,
From Typhus Fever
Brought on from sitting in school
in damp clothes,
After playing at football,
Universally regretted by his comrades
and by his family.

This tablet was erected by
an affectionate brother.

# ON HARROW HILL

YOUR roses I remember,
Dear hill the lime trees crown;
Now gusts of grey November
Blow keen through Harrow Town
Where the boys pass up and down.

Ah! how my heart yearns after
The days and ways I knew
God bless you for your laughter,
You lads in coats of blue —
The great world waits for you.

I too have laughed and chattered
And lingered in the sun
Where are the dreams that flattered
And faded one by one —
And the things I have not done.

Here, friends, when Time shall sever
The thread that binds us yet,
When sleep shall quell endeavour
And night shall drown regret,
I'll rest me and forget.

So gentle hearts and tender,
Lay me my love beside,
Where we may catch the splendour
The gold of eventide
Flooding the pastures wide;

And up from the western meadows
May hear your voices call,
Where Silence is Queen of the shadows
Beside the old Church wall,
And Hope is lord of all.

LOUIS MORIARTY

In early days, Harrow was covered by forests full of oak and hornbeam. Stags, roebuck and wild boar abounded and Harrow was a favourite hunting-ground of the Archbishops of Canterbury and the Kings of England.

The Archbishop's Deer at Harrow ~
"Willelmus rex Goisfredo viscomiti et ceteris Lundoniensibus fidelibus suis salutem. Mando et præcipio vobis ne in terris Lanfranci archiepiscopi, quæ ad Hergam suum manerium pertinent, cervas vel cervos ne capreolas capiatis nec omnino aliquam venationem in eis faciatis præter eos quibus ipse præceperit, vel licentiam dederit."

"King William to Geoffrey, Sheriff, and to all other his faithful citizens of London sendeth greeting. I hereby order and admonish you, that on the lands of Lanfranc the Archbishop, which belong to his manor of Harrow, ye chase neither stags nor hinds nor fallow deer, nor hunt at all on them, except so far as he may order or permit."

This charter must have been issued whilst Lanfranc held the Archbishopric, that is to say, between the years AD 1070 and AD 1090.

———————— • ————————

In 1206 King John gave an order for the maintenance of ten greyhounds and their attendants at Harrow.

———————— • ————————

The King's Head is traditionally the successor of a hunting lodge belonging to Henry VIII. There were few oaks left by then. They had been cut for the erection of All Souls College, Oxford by the Rector of Harrow, John Byrkhede – the same man who built the spire.

" ...and that the woods were grievously devastated by reason of the timber having been felled for the building of the College of the Lord Henry Chichele, the late Archbishop, at Oxford."

( COURT ROLL 1445 )

In April 1646, King Charles I rode through Harrow with two companions. They halted on the Hill and watered their horses at the well.

CHARLES ~ *We'll water horses here. 'Tis Harrow Hill I oft have seen from Windsor. Time was lost at Hillingdon; no word of message came from friend or foe. We are indeed alone!*

THE REVEREND DR. BUSSELL

NEAR THIS SPOT ON 27TH APRIL 1646 KING CHARLES I WHEN FLEEING FROM OXFORD WITH TWO COMPANIONS ON HIS WAY TO SURRENDER TO THE SCOTTISH ARMY AT SOUTHWELL RESTED TO TAKE A LAST LOOK AT LONDON AND TO WATER HIS HORSES AT THE SPRING WHICH STILL RUNS BELOW AND HAS EVER SINCE BEEN CALLED KING CHARLES'S WELL

DANIEL DEFOE mentions in 'A Tour through England and Wales' that:

'On the right hand as we ride from London to Uxbridge, or to Colebrook, we see Harrow, a little town on a very high hill, and is therefore called Harrow on the Hill: The church of this town standing upon the summit of the hill, and having a very handsome and high spire, they tell us, King Charles II, ridiculing the warm disputes among some critical scripturallists of those times, concerning the visible church of Christ upon earth; us'd to say of it, that if there was e'er a visible church upon earth, he believ'd this was one'.

The farmer meanwhile rejoiced in the fertility of the soil. The best corn near London came from Harrow.
"Harrow Hill is the highest in the county, under which lies fruitful fields, especially about Heston (doubtless Headstone), which yields such fine flour that the King's bread was formerly made thereof, and Queen Elizabeth received no money from these villages, but took her wheat in kind for her own use..."

R. BURTON

Admirable Curiosities... 1682

Michael Drayton, who lived between 1563 and 1631 wrote 'A Pastoral', which begins:

This said, the aged street sagged sadly on alone:
And Ver, upon his course, now hasted to be gone
T'accompany his Colne: which as she gently glides,
Doth kindly him embrace: whom soon this hap betides
As Colne come on along, and chanc'd to cast her eye,
Upon that neighbouring Hill where Harrow stands so high,
She Peryvale perceived prank't up with wreaths of wheat
And with exulting terms thus glorying in her feat;
Why should not I be coy, and of my Beauties nice
Since this my goodly grain is held of greatest price?
No manchet can so well the courtly palace please
As that made of the meal fetch'd from my fertile Leas
The finest of that kind, compared with my wheat,
For whiteness of the Bread, doth look like common Cheate.
What Barley is there found, whose fair and bended ear
Makes stouter English Ale, or stronger English Beer?
The Oat, the Bean, and Peas, with me but Pulses are;
The coarse and browner Rye, no more than Fitch and Tare,
What seed doth any soil, in England bring, that I,
Beyond her most increase yet cannot multiply?

Norden, writing in 1573, gives this account:

It may be noted how nature hath exalted that high Harrow on the Hill, as it were in the way of ostentation to shew it selfe to all passengers to and from London, who beholding the same may saye it is the centre (as it were) of the pure vale; for Harrow standeth invironed with a greater contrye of moste pure grounds, from which hill, towardes the time of harveste a man maye beholde the feyldes rounde about so sweetly to address themselves to the sicle and syth, with such comfortable haboundaunce of all kinde of grayne, that it maketh the inhabitants, to clappe theyr handes for joye to see theyr valleys so to laugh and singe.

Yet this fruiteful and pleasante country yeldeth little comforte unto the wayfaringe man in the winter season, by reason of the clayish nature of the soyle, which after it hath tasted the autombe showers it beginneth to mix deep and dirtye, yeldinge unsavery passage to horse and man. Yet the countrye swayne holdeth it a sweet and pleasant garden, and with his whippe and whysell, can make himself melodye, and dance knee deepe in dirte, the whole daye, not holding it any disgrace unto his person.

Such is the force of hope of future proffitt.

> The deepe and dirtiest lothsome soil
> Yeldes golden grayne to carefull toyle.

And that is the cause that the industrious and painful husbandmen will refuse a pallace, to droyle in theys golden puddles.

# The Dirge
## of the Crown and Anchor
## by One of Its Devotees

The tears is a-rolling all down on mi cheek,
Them tears as I'm blowed as they vont let
                                        me speek,
And pail is mi wisage and coold is mi' 'art,
And dry is mi mouth vith the sobs vich vill
                                        start,
For the fates is adwerse ~ vich I guv 'em mi curse,
For thu've doomed thee to death ~ they vas allus
                                        purwurse.

Agin thre hondred years ~ all but tin I may say~
Thou 'as lifted thy 'ead from the bold 'Arra
                                        clay;
Agin thre hundred years have thi chease and
                                        thi beer,
Bin the bow-hideall of our 'Arra gud cheer
Vich I vow and proclame 'tis a blagardly
                                        shame
To banish from 'Arra thisilf and thi name.

Yalla and starn dos the Hanker and Crown
From the crist of the 'ill on its fellers luk
                                        down,

33

'Tis the pride o' the village, the 'ome of its
                                        bliss,
O, vere shall I fin' such anither as this.
May they drink soap and vater ven they cant
                                git her porter,
May they veep and lamint for the sorra thu've
                                brot her.

———— • ————

For generations of boys the Crown and Anchor was
familiarly known as "The Abode of Bliss" from the
name of its proprietor.
Bought by the School in 1862 to be used as the official
dwelling of the School Custos, it was demolished later,
in 1883.

———— • ————

The King's Head was described in 1850 as the principal Hotel of Harrow on the Hill. It was a posting
house with livery and bait stables and horses were
kept for hire.

# PRIVATE AND CONFIDENTIAL.

*To the Editor of Punch.*

SIR,                                              *May 6th,* 1844.

Under any other circumstance than the one I am about to allude to,
I would not for a moment condescend to address you ; but my connexion
with a young lady (in fact, the object of my affections), renders it impera-
tive that I should take notice of a piece of rudeness which certain persons
was guilty of on Monday the 6th inst.   On the day mentioned, business, or
rather—(for why should I mince matters)—pleasure called me to Arrow-
on-the-Ill.   In the company of her to whom I have already given my eart,
and ope to give my and, I dined at the King's Ead, intending after
dinner to enjoy, with my cigar and my brandy and water, that delightful
conversation which can only grow out of the union of 2 soles, I mean, of
course, love.   Mary Ann and me retired from the dinner-table to the
beautiful gardens adjacent to the house, and seated on a rustic bench,
enjoying the beauties of nature, we were almost as appy as two engaged
ones could be, when we was—were, I mean—disturbed by shouts of laughter
coming from a certain party.   I was induced to think (and Mary Ann
thought so too), that we were the subjects of their idle merriment.   We
were confirmed in our opinion when we saw a individual take out a sketch-
book and commence (as I suppose) taking off our heads.   Now, sir, what
there could be so amusing in us we cannot see ; but perhaps what the poet
BYRON observes,

> " He jests at scars, who never felt
> The pangs that wait, that wait on love,"

will explain it.   In conclusion, let me inform you, sir, that in my opinion
fun is one thing, and that jesting with the finest feelings of our nature is
another, and am, sir, &c.,

*Islington.*                                    AUGUSTUS BANGS.

[Can the above have reference to the preceding sketch, which has been
forwarded to us anonymously ?—*Ed. of Punch.*]

## HARROW TREES

Trees, and trees! Roam where you will:
Oak in the meadow, elm on the hill,
And in leafy June, in Grove and Copse,
A whispered spell in the tall tree tops.
Fragrant limes on their stately guard,
And the grand old cedar, tempest-scarred,
Where the silvery spire, o'er woodland and lea,
Is a beacon set for the world to see.

But the crown and glory of Harrow is still,
The lordly Beech on the crest of the hill,
Where the sloping highway, winding down,
Faces the tide of London town.
There it stands, like a sentry set
By a city gate, on the parapet
Straight the sheer stem, and overhead
Is a world of leaves like waters shed,
When the palace fountain skyward springs
On some festal day, in a garden of kings.

LOUIS MORIARTY (1921)

36

## A LAMENT

The stately Beech, the pride of Harrow hill,
That some were fain to love and all to praise,
Stands slowly dying. Gone the leafy maze,
Blighted and seared by some insidious ill.
The Things that perish! Ah, how oft they fill
Our lives with beauty and, in mystic ways,
Speak their own speech throughout the
                    changing days
And touch our hearts and hallowed memory
                         still.

Long ages past, when Nature was divine,
When Nymph and Dryad haunted every glade,
The simple folk, with honey, milk, and wine,
To their lost friend due offering had made.
We dimly feel a grace, a splendour fled —
Have we no word to say, no tear to shed?

*LOUIS MORIARTY (1928)*

37

When the afternoon is over
And the evening brings the breeze,
And the sunset glories hover
Round the steeple and the trees,
In the twilight as the shadows
Come to meet us o'er the plain,
We will wander thro' the meadows
Up the Hill and home again.

# THE
# SCHOOL
## ON THE HILL

"Five hundred faces, and all so strange!
Life in front of me ~ home behind.
I felt like a waif before the wind
Tossed on an ocean of shock and change."

# FOUNDATION

On this most noble height
Unmoved by time,
Still centre of a spectrum of delight
Played through in brilliant light
With measured chime;
Uplifted by the upward pointing spire
To selfless, true and visionary desire,
A virtuous founder destiny obeyed,
As law and honour he for framework laid,
And built a school.

No mean dimension he as yardstick held
But put to service all that he beheld —
This being his land,
The faithful steward rendered back the gift

Penned statute strong with discipline to sift
The fine from coarse;
Judged with the visionary's inward eye
The length and breadth,
Then held it firm.
How sweet and strong that first-formed single
sound

That later orchestrations built around,
Yet still the note transcends and guides the whole,
Quickening the heart.
Alluring sound beguiles the wanderer,
Calls forth response and feeds the thirsty soul,
Brings peace and meaning to the daily life.

DOROTHY BOUX

HEARE LYETH BVRYED THE BODYE OF JOHN LYON LATE OF PRESTON
IN THIS PISH YEOMAN DECEASED THE iii TH DAYE OF OCTOBER
IN THE YEARE OF OVR LORD 1592. WHO HATH FOVNDED A FREE
GRAMMER SCHOOLE IN THIS PISH TO HAVE CONTINVANCE
FOR EVER AND FOR MAINTENAVNCE THEREOF AND FOR RELLEYFE
OF THE POORE AND OF SOME POORE SCHOLLERS IN THE VNIVERS
SITYES REPAYRINGE OF HIGH WAYES , AND OTHER GOOD AND
CHARITABLE VSES HATH MADE CONVAYAVNCE OF LANDS OF
GOOD VALVE TO A CORPORACION GRAVNTED FOR THAT PVRPOSE
PRAYSE BE TO THE AVTHOR OF AL GOODNES WHO MAKE VS
MYNDEFVLL TO FOLLOWE HIS GOOD EXAMPLE

Long before John Lyon obtained a Royal Charter for his Free Grammar School, there was a school on the Hill which occupied a building known as Church House that was situated near the churchyard.

Queen Mary had sent some of her protégés there –

Bridgewater
May 26,1626.

To my worshipful Cozen,
   ... I and my 5 brethren were all borne in Hide Park by London in the Lodge neere Knightsbridge. My Father's name was Richard hee was servant to King Henry VII and to King Henry VIII and was a Pentioner and much in their favor as I have heard my Mother and many others say...
   I was not above 8 or 9 years old when he died as I take it. I remember Queen Mary came into our house within a little of my Father's death and ffound my mother weeping and took her by the hand and lifted her up – for she neeled – and bad her bee of good cheer for her children sh' bee well provided for.

Afterwards my brother Rᵒ and I being the two eldest were sent to Harrow to school and were there till we were almost men.

G. ROPER

———•———

There are also records at Caius College, Cambridge with the names of entrants who had been at the school at Harrow before 1571.

———•———

The pre-Lyonian school was certainly ecclesiastical. When in 1545 the connection between the Hill and Canterbury was severed the school must have fallen on hard times and languished.

Queen Elizabeth, like Edward VI, encouraged the foundation and restoration of free grammar schools and during her reign many endowments were made by merchants, country gentry and others.

———•———

VIVAT REGINA

Elizabeth R̄ gr'a
At Court ~ John Lyon's
Charter

(Queen Elizabeth seated and
surrounded by Courtiers
and Ladies dressed for a revel. Enter Sir Gilbert Gerard
bearing a parchment roll, and followed by John Lyon,
who remains in the background, while Gerard advances
to the throne.)

QUEEN ~ *Good morrow, Master Attorney! But why
dost thou bring us business today, to mar our
revels?*

GERARD ~ *Madam, you did appoint me this day
to usher into your presence a humble suitor.
We spoke of his business but lately.*

QUEEN ~ *And is that thy suitor yonder, whose
sober garb but ill accords with our gala Court?
We dislike such kill-joy interludes to merriment.
And yet the good man's simple gravity constrains
attention. Well, bring him forward and remind
us of his affair.*

GERARD ~ *'Tis one John Lyon, a trusty yeoman*

45

who owns broad lands at Preston in the Parish of Harrow and elsewhere. Of his substance he relieves the poor and supports some thirty poor scholars of his parish. For these, and for other pupils beyond his parish, he would establish and endow for ever a free Grammar School, to be incorporated by this royal charter, which I have here engrossed and ready for your sign manual. May it please your Highness to grant his suit?

(Lyon is brought forward.)

QUEEN ~ So, Master Lyon, thou would'st found a School at Harrow. But have we not heard of scholars educated there already? Did not our sister, the late Queen Mary, support sundry pensioners at a School on "Mons, the Hill"?

LYON ~ True, Madam, but it hath fallen on evil days and is like to perish. I would fain renew it on a lasting foundation; and for that purpose I would devote all my substance, when my wife and I shall have departed, for the erection of a fair building, to house both scholars and their teachers.

QUEEN ~ But why, Master Lyon, build housing for scholars whose homes are close at hand?

LYON ~ May it please your Highness, I would not only benefit my neighbours, but would

attract so many foreigners as can be conveniently
accommodated by their Master.
QUEEN ~ And how wilt thou draw these foreigners?
LYON ~ By providing them with sound and reli-
gious learning. I would have them attend the
Church and hear godly sermons. They shall be
taught their grammar of the Greek and Latin,
wherein your Highness is herself proficient.
Their morals shall eke be looked to, for the
Master shall prevent all swearing, lying, pick-
ing, fighting, and wantonness of speech. Aye,
and their outward mien shall not be neglected;
for none may come to my school uncombed,
unwashed, ragged or slovenlike. And for the
better access to my seat of learning, I will main-
tain the road from this London to yonder Harrow
in good repair.
QUEEN ~ 'Tis a good scheme, Master Lyon, we
vow. But teach them not only the classic tongues.
For doth not Master Robert Ascham, our Secretary, say "He that will write well in any tongue
must speak as the common people do, and
think as wise men do; so shall every man
understand him, and the judgment of wise men
will follow him " Thou must also teach the lads
to shoot, that they may make us good soldiers
in these troublous days.

47

LYON ~ Madam, I have provided that every Harrow boy shall bring to school a bow and shafts to practise archery.

QUEEN ~ But how wilt thou ensure that thy wishes be observed in after years?

GERARD ~ My liege, this good old friend, Master Lyon, hath appointed Keepers and Governors, whereof myself am one. 'Twill be for us to execute his will and husband his estate for the welfare of his School.

QUEEN ~ A great trust, sir! Be thou and thy successors ever loyal thereto. Be your motto "Donorum Dei Dispensatio Fidelis". Our late brother, Edward, hath founded many a fair grammar-school in our land; and one of our Royal Predecessors, the sixth Henry, hath left to our College of Eton the glory of his name. For ourselves, we would not rob thee of thy credit as Founder of thy School; yet we rejoice that our name should be linked with this new cradle of learning, however humble in its origin. But we presage for it a noble destiny...

Thus shall thy School rank with the foundations of Wykeham and Royal Henry, and its fame shall spread as far as the sails of our bold sea-rover, trusty Drake. Therefore, Master Attorney, thy pen, and we will sign this charter. And thou, Master Lyon, take it with God's blessing on thy generous intent. So fare thee well! And now let our Court address itself to the revel which we have thus profitably delayed.

(Exit LYON, with the roll)

E. GRAHAM
(Harrow Historical Pageant, 1923)

Whereas our beloved subject, John Lyon, of Preston, within the parish of Harrowe-upon-the-Hill... hath purposed in his mind a certain grammar school and one schoolmaster and usher within the village of Harrowe-upon-the-Hill of new to erect found and for ever to establish for the perpetual education, teaching and instruction of children and youth... Do will, grant and ordain for us, our heirs and successors that there for ever hereafter there be and shall be one grammar school in the village of Harrowe-upon-the-Hill...

FROM THE CHARTER

# HARROW

The holy spire that tapers to the blue,—
The guardian elms whose vesper shadows fall
On turf and tomb,— the many-lettered wall,
Carven of hands once manful to pursue
Their daily toil of honest things and true,—
The ample stair, the street, the field, they all
With voiceless magic eloquence recall
A fragrance of dead days, when life was new.
Yet here,'mid laughter and the ring of cheers,
Immortal Boyhood keeps his joyous throne;
With daring eyes aflame and eager ears
He burns for conquest of a world unknown.
O stay thee, lonely pilgrim of the years,—
Here at the heart of Youth revive thine own.

Harrow! not thine the vows of saintly king,
Nor purple-garbéd Prelate's fostering pride;
Thy lowly yeoman Founder strove and died,
Unwitting what the wondrous years would bring~
What brave procession of thy sons would spring,
To quell the stranger foe, and sweep the tide:
Or glow with patriot faith, and greatly guide
Our equal England, ~ poet-souls to fling
From earth to sky their songs defiant dart,
And scholars inward-eyed: yet, chance what may,
We shall not come less humbly to thy shrine,
Knowing that homespun story; risen thou art
From that pale dawn to this thy perfect day;
Our flickering lights but win their fire from
                                    thine.

LORD CREWE
1898

51

*Ida! blest spot, where Science holds her reign,*

*How joyous once I join'd thy youthful train!*

BYRON

52

# ON A DISTANT VIEW OF THE VILLAGE AND SCHOOL, OF HARROW ON THE HILL

Ye scenes of my childhood, whose lov'd recollection,
Embitters the present, compar'd with the past;
Where science first dawn'd on the powers of
                                    reflection,
And friendships were form'd, too romantic to last.

Where fancy, yet, joys to retrace the resemblance,
Of comrades, in friendship and mischief allied;
How welcome to me, your ne'er fading remembrance,
Which rests in the bosom, though hope is deny'd!

Again I revisit the hills where we sported,
The streams where we swam, and the fields where
                                    we fought;
The school, where loud warn'd, by the bell, we
                                    resorted,
To pore o'er the precepts by Pedagogues taught.

Again I behold, where for hours I have ponder'd,
As reclining, at eve, on yon tombstone I lay;
Or round the steep brow of the churchyard I
                                    wander'd,
To catch the last gleam of the sun's setting ray.

I once more view the room, with spectators surrounded,
Where, as Zanga, I trod on Alonzo o'erthrown;
While, to swell my young pride, such applauses
                                        resounded,
I fancied that Mossop himself was outshone.

Or, as Lear, I pour'd forth the deep imprecation,
By my daughters, of kingdom and reason depriv'd;
Till, fir'd by loud plaudits, and self adulation,
I regarded myself, as a Garrick reviv'd.

Ye dreams of my boyhood, how much I regret you,
Unfaded your memory dwells in my breast;
Though sad and deserted, I ne'er can forget you,
Your pleasures may still be, in fancy, possest.

To Ida, full oft may remembrance restore me,
While Fate shall the shades of the future unroll,
Since Darkness o'er shadows the prospect before me,
More dear is the beam of the past to my soul.

But, if through the course of the years which await me
Some new scene of pleasure should open to view,
I will say, while with rapture the thought shall
                                        elate me,
"Oh! such were the days, which my infancy knew."

LORD BYRON
(Hours of Idleness ~ 1806)

# A JUNE EVENING
## AT HARROW

Six of the clock,
And from the hum of bill
The laughing crowds lounge
on their homeward way,
Five hundred voices rise above the
Hill,
One boasts his little triumph of the day,
And lingers on his score with fond delay;
While this his eyes in sudden spell hath cast
Where Phyllis sets betimes her proud array
Of great straw pottles red with juice, and vast
With luscious berries; these his eventide
repast.

Seven of the clock. And from the churchyard height
One cloud I see in snowy mountains rolled;
Each over each melts into creamy white
Hard by the edges tinged to gradual gold;
And earth is bright with colour thousandfold.
And far below I hear the sounding ball
Click on the bat: almost my ear hath told
Each well-known voice, and the familiar call,
So stilly all around doth solemn even fall.

Eight of the clock. And silence glideth down,
Sweet smells of even fan the quiet street;
With pleasant converse through the hushful town
Two chance companions stroll with lazy feet;
Anon in mirthful mood they passing greet
The jocund tradesman at his door, or hail
The batsmen homeward wending, or repeat
Some old scholastic legendary tale; and far
In the deep heavens the evening star doth pale.

Nine of the clock. And through th'impervious bars
I hear the homeward rustic's rude "Goodnight,"
As, pipe enkindling 'neath propitious stars,
He blows the dusky gloaming into light,
And his brown face with ruddy glow is bright;
Far down the stony street I hear him tread
Waking the silent haunts. So out of sight

To his scant meal he goes, and humble bed,
And all around the dark mysterious vail is spread.

Ten of the clock. Far out on Hampstead Hill
The lights are flickering. Very chill and cold
The night breeze at my window. All is still,
Save when the great old sycamore doth hold
His low love story, as he would enfold
The night in his embrace. But ghostly white,
As round the isles the ancient seas are rolled,
The mists are silvered in the pale moonlight
About the silent hills. Goodnight, a last
                              goodnight.

ANON — 1861

57

# UP THE HILL
## A Song of Harrow ~

Oh, it's good to be at Harrow, in boyhood's
golden day,
It's good to be at Harrow, when the heart is blithe
and gay;
It's good to learn life's lessons there -with other
"flanneled fools",
To play with other "muddied oafs", to vie with
other schools;
It's good to read and mark and learn and inwardly
digest
Old Cicero and Sophocles and Plato and the rest;
But this is best -in all to strive our duty to fulfil,
While we are boys at Harrow, at Harrow-on-the-Hill.

Oh, it's bitter leaving Harrow, when at last the
end is here,
Oh, hard it is to bid farewell to all we hold so dear;
Remembering the golden days that cannot come
again,
Descending to life's conflict with the people of
the plain.
How much it was we meant to do, how little we
have done!

How weak the struggles we have made, how few the
                                battles won!
Oh, fare you well, you others, who our places here
                                will fill,
As we pass away with heavy hearts from Harrow
                                down the hill.


There's a bigger world than Harrow and its hills
                                are steep and high,
And it's none too easy climbing them, however
                                hard we try;
And often we shall falter, and often we shall fail,
And sometimes all our efforts will appear of no avail
But if we've learnt our lesson, and are true to
                                Harrow's name,
In larger fields than Harrow's we will always play
                                the game
And set our teeth, determined, with heart, and
                                mind, and will,
Through all our lives for Harrow's sake to struggle
                                up the hill.


ANON ~ 1907

*... I have provided that every Harrow boy shall bring to school a bow and shafts to practise archery...   (John Lyon).*

## THE SILVER ARROW

In 1684 Sir Gilbert Talbot gave a silver arrow to be competed for at an archery meeting.

It became an important annual school function, taking place on the first Thursday of August, but in 1761, changed to the first Thursday of July.

The competitors, originally six, later twelve, were attired in fancy dresses of spangled satin, the usual colours being white and green: they also wore green silk sashes and silken caps.

The boys shot ten arrows each; a 'bull' was greeted with a concert of French horns. The victor carried the silver arrow home, a triumphal procession of boys attending him.

The day ended with a ball to which the neigh-bouring gentry were invited. The last silver arrow contest took place in 1771. It had become too popular and was drawing disorderly crowds from London. Speech Day was instituted in its place.

And there, encased, the guerdon erst of Harrow,
    Now the rembrancer of former fame,
    Reposes in due state the Silver Arrow,
That taught each youthful archer 'twas foul shame
To miss the mark, much more to take false aim
    At life's great target, swerving into sin:
    Now bows no more, but mimic battles claim
    Our hero-spirits, and the martial din
Warns us of future, greater, fights to wage, and win.

WALTER  SYDNEY  SICHEL (1871)

## THE SILVER ARROW

I sing the praise of the olden days,
When yeomen and burghers knew
In the arrow's flight was the Nation's might,
Our strength in the bended yew.
In the Baron's hall there was sport for all,
Tourney, and revel and laugh,
And many a bout had the henchmen stout
With cudgel and quarter staff.

The book is read, and the prayers are said,
Then all to the butts repair,
The men are seen in the jerkin green,
And the maidens are watching there.
Full well they know no foreign foe
Our shores will dare invade,
With pikemen bold our walls to hold,
And archers in every glade.

Their spirit to-day is dead, men say ~
Dead as their stalwart frames ~
Their blood now runs in idler sons,
Loving less manly games.
Can this be truth? Arise, our youth,
Rise in your strength, and show
By word and by deed ye are worthy seed
Of your sires who drew the bow.

(Music ~ PERCY BUCK)                    C. J. MALTBY (1910)

*Score Card of the Shooting for the Silver Arrow at Harrow the Hill*

| Names of the Archers for 1769 | And for 1770 | Num° of shoots | Names of the Archers for 1769 | And for 1770 | Num° of Shoots |
|---|---|---|---|---|---|
| Mr Whitmore | Mr Lemon | | Mr Leigh | Mr Lewis | |
| Mr Lemon | Mr Tighe | | Mr Tunstall | Rt Hon Lᵈ Rawdon | |
| Mr Maclean | Mr Watkins | | Mr Jones | Mr Franks | |
| Mr Tighe | Mr Leigh | | Mr Merry | Mr Allen | |
| Mr Watkins | Mr Tunstall | | Mr Yatman | Mr Crosbie | |
| Mr Poyntz | Mr Powell | | Mr Franks | Mr Merry | |

# CRICKET AT HARROW

*" I claim for our cricket ground a share, and a very considerable share too, in the foundation of the character of an English gentleman."*

ROBERT GRIMSTON

The early archives are absolutely silent about the subject of cricket. But with the abolition of the Silver Arrow contest and the establishment of the Marylebone Cricket Club in 1787, the game of cricket was soon to gain a permanent footing at the school.

In 1805 this challenge was issued to Eton:

Harrow June 20th 1805.

The Gentlemen of Harrow School request the honour of trying their Skill at Cricket with the Gentlemen of Eton, on Wednesday July 31st at Lord's Cricket Ground. A Speedy answer, declaring whether the time and place be convenient, will oblige

The match was played on the old Lord's Ground. After their victory Eton sent the following epigram to Harrow:

"Adventurous 'boys' of Harrow School,
Of cricket you've no knowledge!
Ye played not cricket, but the fool
With men of Eton college!"

Lord Byron, who played in the match, and took one wicket, is said to have written the reply:

"Ye Eton wits, to play the fool
Is not the boast of Harrow School;
No wonder then, at our defeat,
Folly like yours could ne'er be beat!"

The chestnut trees had a history of their own. They were each planted by a member of the cricket XI who had made fifty runs or more in a school match. The boy dug the hole for the tree and repeated the words "I plant this tree" and his score which entitled him to do so. A claret cup was handed round, and three cheers given. It was all done in a very solemn way and it was considered a great honour to have planted a tree. Some of these trees still exist today, such as those near the Bowling shed on the VI th form ground. There are several others near to the Richardson Pavilion on the Phil ground and some on the far side of the Bessborough ground near to the Church Fields. Every tree had a metal tab on it with the name of the boy, and the year when it was planted.

STANLEY A. HAYWOOD

*Professional cricketer to Harrow School 1907-1957*
*Head Groundsman 1920-1957.*

## The Second Eleven —

The 2nd XI was always fun,
Nobody cared if it lost or won,
Whether the pitch was wet or dry
The 2nd XI would always try.

Though some were in white and some
                    were in grey,
The 2nd XI was always gay;
Some had two pads, and some had one;
The 2nd XI was much more fun.

H. CRACROFT WHITE

———— • ————

Read my name upon the panels

Carved in gold along the boards

See myself arrayed in flannels

Batting for the School at Lords.

E. W. HOWSON.

$A$nd so the years pass...

Lord's changes but Lord's remains. From the genial hubbub to the hush that can be felt, the hush in which no sound is heard but the intaken breath, the patter of the bowler's feet to the crease, the ball against the bat, how unchanging is each phase of the everchanging game! There we still may meet old friends, from home and from all corners of the earth: there is the game we have all played with varying success, but whose spirit still inspires us. There are the boys, eternal, and with them, never to be forgotten, the little sisters, eager and partisan, most loyal comrades in weal and woe.

STANLEY BALDWIN (1926)

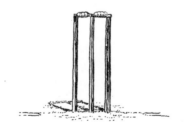

66

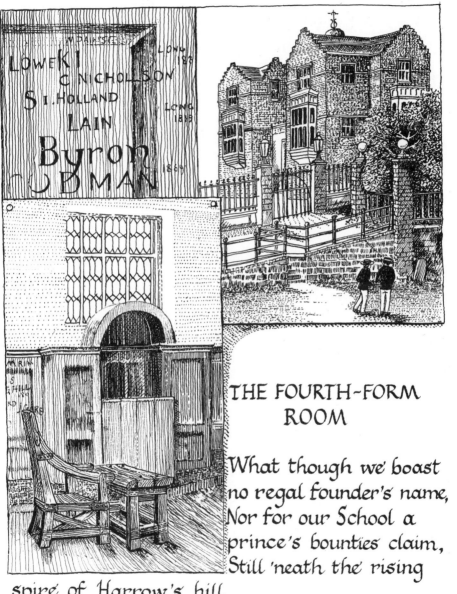

## THE FOURTH-FORM ROOM

What though we boast
no regal founder's name,
Nor for our School a
prince's bounties claim,
Still 'neath the rising
spire of Harrow's hill
Stand true memorial of honour; still
Loved more than Byron's elm and Byron's tomb,
The high-prized glory of our Fourth-Form Room.

The Fourth-Form Room! aye, by the very word
A cord is touched, a pride deep-rooted stirred,
No less in him who but this quarter came,
Proud in that room to answer to his name,
Than him who boasts with pride a second year,
And talks of new boys with contemptuous
                                        sneer.

Mark the bare walls, which jealous time hath
                                        scarred,
The benches rude, by ink and gashes marred,
Read but those names before thou quit the
                                        scene,
Of those who now are not, but erst have been,
Carved there in careless mood by boyish hand,-
They now sleep, honoured by a grateful Father-
                                        land.

Oh, what more pure desire for pure renown
Than when 'mongst names like these we leave
                                        our own,
Inscribed with them on these time-honoured walls,
In the old place which fancy oft recalls,
That one in after years may point out ours,
                                        and tell,
He, once at Harrow, honoured Harrow well.

ANON (1860)

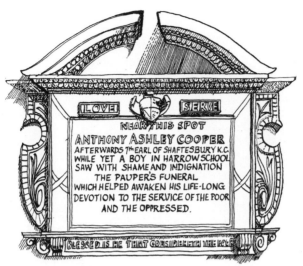

Peer and Patrician—Shaftesbury shines
Great in an age that belonged to the Great,
An age that recked naught of the Small,
Worshipping Power!
He stood, as a boy, in the Yard on the Hill;
He saw a mean coffin crash hard to the ground.
From that moment he vowed to devote his young life
To champion the helpless.
Philanthropy turned him from child into priest;
Priest, aye, and prophet foreseeing the day
When claims then denied and deemed almost unclean
Should be granted as Rights.
Scholar and born in the purple, he turned
His face to the many instead of the Few.
So he lives in our hearts, for high on the Hill
He dropped dew on the Plain.

HORACE ANNESLEY VACHELL
(Harrow Historical Pageant ~ 1923)

69

## ON HARROW TERRACE

Behind ~ the old Elizabethan school,
Chapel and formroom clustering in the trees,
A little world of academic rule
Busy and restless as a hive of bees;
Where ordered work and simple worship blend,
Thought marries thought, and friend is knit with friend.

Below ~ the meadows, fields of happy fight,
Rich with the memory of a thousand frays,
Where rival forces clash in fierce delight,
And boyhood plucks its first and proudest bays.
Oh joy of mimic battle! generous feud!
Rough nurse of freedom, strength and fortitude.

Beyond - the mighty city spreading far,
Smoke-wrapt, mysterious, pinnacle and spire,
Big with tremendous fates that make or mar
A scene to strike the soul of youth afire —
Great London looming black against the night,
Silent, beneath her lurid belt of light!

O boys! O men that will be! yonder lies
The world before you. Forth, and play your parts!
Your Country calls for valiant sons and wise,
Quick brains, intrepid wills, and loyal hearts.
So shall your Founder's motto thrive and grow—
  "DONORUM DEI DISPENSATIO"

EDMUND WHYTEHEAD HOWSON (1898)

## Adieu to Harrow

*Written on the author leaving school*

At length the wish'd~for day's arriv'd, that day
Which Fancy pictur'd oft in bright array;
When every thought~swoln trouble would be o'er,
And Greek and Latin clog the brain no more;
When joys awaited, numberless to tell,
And scenes where varied pleasures ever dwell...

My Arnold, shall I quit, unnotic'd, you,
Without one thought, one kind, one last adieu!
A tender sprig intrusted to your care,
You screen'd the sapling from the winter's air;
Full many a fag I 'scap'd up Harrow Hill;

By you protected from the tyrant's will;
Accept then, here, the greeting of my heart,
'Tis Custom's laws compel me to depart.
Adieu, sweet Grove! beneath whose spreading shade
I oft invok'd the Muses' friendly aid:
Oft there, with plodding gait, I've paus'd along,
When study forc'd me from the playful throng:
And you, stern lion! who with roaring voice,
My slumbers broke, and made me curse thy noise.

And now my friends, — but hark! the calling bell,
Yet one more hearty squeeze, and then farewell!
I go to steer my bark on dang'rous seas,
And dread the russle of each slender breeze:
Yet fill'd with thy best cheer, in hopes I fail,
And gather strength against th' impending gale:
Then fare-ye-well, tho' sure in leaving you,
To real happiness I bid adieu!

SAVILLON.   (1795)

## On a
## Distant View of Harrow School

*Written at Windsor*

Hail! sweet remembrancer of former days,
Thou kind reflector of my early youth;
Beneath whose learned roof I sought for praise
And trod the way to knowledge and to truth.

Alas! ye hills, ye dales, dear haunts of play!
Ye social walks within yon sacred bow'r,
Where oft I pictur'd many a happy day,
And drew false prospects of the future hour.

Where now those friends that swore eternal love,
Those ties which bound our blended souls in one;
Those vows, then made sincerity to prove,
E'er vice or pride to sway the heart begun.
Gone are those friends – like visions now they seem,
And nought remains but Life's delusive dream.

*SAVILLON 1795*

74

# THE ADIEU

Written under the impression
that the author
would soon die

Adieu, thou Hill! where early joy
Spread roses o'er my brow;
Where Science seeks each loitering boy
With knowledge to endow.
Adieu my youthful friends or foes,
Partners of former bliss or woes;
No more through Ida's paths we stray;
Soon must I share the gloomy cell,
Where ever-slumbering inmates dwell
Unconscious of the day.

LORD   BYRON
1807

75

# REVISITED

In careless wise we left thee, ignorant
Of gracious and peculiar privilege.
We said: The wide world calls us masterful,
With vision of her vast humanity.
With voices of her million-minded cities
And shoutings of her heavily-rolling sea,
She calls, insistent and deliberate.
Goodbye, we said: we will go out to her.
In careless wise we left thee, ignorant,
And thou didst let us go: but memory
Is stronger than that million-minded world,
Whose bells are weaker than thy harmonies,
Weaker her loud and lamentable waves.
Slowly with golden cords thou didst assay
To draw us back to thee: with golden cords,
Yea, thou didst draw us back. O beautiful,
Spire-crowned and lifted into clearest air,
Mother of blue horizons, dear and great,
A little while we saw thy face again.

Thine eyes are wells profound of memory,
We were refreshed with looking into them:
The days long distant walked beside our feet,
And followed us out into the empty earth.

Yea, changelessly, old hill immutable,
For us thou waitest, even as Sion waits
For all the labouring kindreds of the world,
Across the sea-wave of eternity,
Honourable, with amethystine pinnacles,
And final bourne of weary wayfarings.
Thou waitest. Always may we have return.
And though away, be in thy memory,
Held to thee by a strong and golden chain,
Far sundered exiles, but thy children still.

WILFRED ROWLAND CHILDE

**O**ur House is built of hearts, not stony walls

**A**nd thus can change not, till the breasts of all

**T**hat love her throb no more: when England falls,

**A**nd not till then, shall ancient Harrow fall.

**A**s clustering ivy clings to sheltering hall,

**H**arrow to England clings, and time for both

**H**as served but to cement the embrace, and call

**F**rom out each century a greener growth;

**A**nd fresher shoots, and livelier leafage still she
showeth.

WALTER SYDNEY SICHEL · 1871

POR · VALOUR

1837-38    W. PEEL 1854

A.R.DUNN, 1854

Names neat in line and regiment

J.W CHAPLIN 1860

Graven in order stark,

GIFFORD 1874

History become an invoice,    1879

P. SMARLING 1884

Valour a mason's mark .CONGREVE 1899

So few? the eye may count them
With scarce a minute lost —
And never mark behind them
The huge unnumbered host.

Their names, complete, compacted,
So short the tale they spell?
Their names? Their names are legion;
Their tale no heart can tell.

So cold? so lost to living
In the stone-vaulted night
From all the blaze of being
From all that stirs delight.

No, name on name they beckon
Up from the prisoning lines
And point us past our twilight
To where the sun still shines.

R.W. MOORE

Six hundred and forty six
Harrovians gave their lives during the Great War

## FROM FLANDERS
Christmas 1915

" I will lift up mine eyes unto
the hills from whence cometh my help"

Soil of the Hill, soil of the Hill
Mother and fount of our myriad streams
We who have life from thee, health from thee, laughter,
Learning (perhaps!) and the splendour of dreams,
Upward we look, in the Fortunes come after
Holpen we look to Thee, helping us still,
Soil of the Hill, soil of the Hill.

Soil of the Plain, soil of the Plain
Terror by night and despair of the morn
We who have loss from thee, utter denying,
Anguish of body, benumbéd and torn —
Up to the Hill in her strength of undying
Look we and laugh and are certain again,
Soil of the Plain, soil of the Plain.

God of the Hill, God of the Plain
Marshal of us, going out, coming in,
We who have life from Thee, praise Thee for living,
Thee for the Hill that has helped us to win,
Praise Thee for plains that we won in the giving
Back unto Thee, Thine ensample of pain,
God of the Hill, God of the Plain.

E.M.W

( Eric Milner~White )

# FROM THE DARDANELLES

There's no one living at Harrow who understands
what I feel,
For my heart is still at Harrow though I live in a ship
of steel,
My heart is always at Harrow, though I serve my King
on the sea —
But there's no one living at Harrow now, who cares two
straws for me!

For him whom most I honoured God has called to his rest,
His place may soon forget him, but never the souls he
blessed,
And, God be thanked! he learned my love, and the debt
I could ne'er repay,
For I saw him and spoke to him of it before he was called
away;
'T was good, 't was good, to feel his prayers which followed
me through the sea —
But there's no one living at Harrow now, who prays a
prayer for me.

There was another at Harrow, a year and a year ago
Whose name I held in the honour that only schoolboys know.
The honour 'twixt boy and Master, whose lives fall much
together

In School and House and Play, in fair and cloudy weather.
But his life is a ransom for Europe's liberty,
And there's no one living at Harrow now, who cares
                                two straws for me.

Oh, when a mail from England reaches our war-worn
                                ship,
Glad is the heart with a gladness one may not tell
                                with the lip;
Scanning the lettered pages welcomed with anxious joy,
"Fallen in Battle", one reads a name that one loved as
                                a boy;
There on the mainland fighting, as I have fought on the
                                sea,
Passed to their death the comrades who made my
                                Harrow for me!

Faces of Friends I loved! Faces of boys I knew!
What is left me of Harrow since God hath taken you?
Still stands the Hill of yore, crowned with the
                                Schools and the spire,
Still at his feet there stretches the wonderful rolling
                                shire ~
Still from the yard at "Bill" the "River flows to the Sea"~
But there isn't a soul among them who cares two
                                straws for me!

                DARDANELLES - September 16th, 1915.

## March 1915

We got up at 4 a.m. yesterday, marched a few miles and then spent the rest of the day waiting for orders. That is rather tiring work and I found myself repeatedly asking myself what I would be doing if I was at Harrow. What time I usually got into first school (7.28 punctually, you know) we were marching along a very muddy road listening to our guns bombarding splendidly, with aeroplanes dashing to and fro overhead. What time I go forth to play fives. a batch of German prisoners came by ...

So you are back again for the dear old summer term, and the garden is bright with flowers.

How have my friends the tulips done, the glorious red ones? I could do with a quiet day in the sun there with nothing to worry me.

I see you still have strikes. That on top of the Russian reverses is rather depressing to read. But as long as no one in England talks about peace till we have won ~ really won ~ all is well. The next generation must be spared the horrors of modern war. All of us out here are ready to go through with it but we have rather a haunting fear that the people (or the politicians) at home, perhaps even out of misplaced pity for us, may be willing to call it a draw. If you lose <u>all</u> your friends don't tolerate a draw.

I shall think of you all rallying on the Old Hill this week. I have tried to do my best for it according to my lights. No one can say what a future lies before it after the war. But it is grand to think of the great response it has made to the war's appeal. And I shall be proud and happy to be among "the old Harrovians who fell in the great war".


CHARLES EYRE


Six days later, leading his company, he was first into the barbed wire and was there shot through the head.

# HARROW'S HONOUR

"Let us now praise famous men."

A weary time, a dreary time, a time of hopes
and fears,
The weeks that pass, the months that pass, and
lengthen into years,
My heart goes back to Harrow, to Harrow far
away,
And Harrow sends a message to cheer me on
my way.
"For good come, bad come, they came the same
before,
So heigh ho, follow the game, and show the way
to more."

Mourn not for those whose names are writ
in gold,
They fought for England, gladly gave their all.
Kept Harrow's honour spotless as of old,
Nor feared to answer to the last great call.

They showed the way to more, their names will
ring,
Through all succeeding years of Harrow's fame,

Whatever changes after years may bring
Their sons will follow up and play the game.

O Mother Herga, all our thanks we give
For all your care of us, your watchful eye;
You made us men, you taught us how to live
And in your wisdom taught us how to die.

The strongest bond of all, the bond of friends
Made in our youth, a bond that none can
                              break,
Binds us to you until our journey ends,
We live, we fight, we die for Harrow's sake.

                    J. M. ROSE ~ TROUP.
                    ( Captain, "The Queen's" )


Friedberg in Hessen,
    20th June, 1916.

87

## 1939 ~ 1945

"There will never lack a youth of Britain capable of
facing, enduring, conquering everything in the name of
freedom and for the sake of their dear loved native land."

Winston Churchill ~ Dec.1944

We who were English, young and skilled
To read the lore that England taught,
Laid by our books, went down and fought
And learnt our lesson and were killed.

That task is over. Our concern
Is with another lesson now
But do not ask us what or how;
We cannot tell you. You will learn.

R.W.MOORE.

Stark on the door their roll is writ;
Six steps into the chapel yonder
Walk past the way they guard and sit.
And as you sit let memory wander
Over the years between. Is it
So long a time to ponder?

Thirty years back those others went
(Dark on the farther wall they glimmer)
With eager step and high intent
With heart aglow and mind a-simmer,
On youth and young adventure bent,
Dim names now, memories dimmer.

And we – hereafter shall we turn
To tablets prematurely hoary,
Find vague emotions which concern
King…Country…Sacrifice…and Glory,
Attaching to the storied urn
A predetermined story.

Breathe, as you catch the undertones
Beneath the words memorials borrow,
A prayer that these proud martyr bones
Forgive your penny-alms of sorrow,
Whose bodies are the silent stones
With which we pave our morrow.    R.W.MOORE

Turn back the scorebook, test its spell
Over the fields you knew so well,
Where earlier innings blurred with age
Dance on the pencil-dotted page.

Here through the overs skill and pluck
Wrangled it out with nerve and luck
In runs accounted, hopes undone
Under the gilded August sun.

Read till the giants, white-arrayed,
Wake from a long Lethean shade
And heroes such as legends tell
Stride from the fields of asphodel.

Hear phantom hands applaud the stroke
That cleared the rails, the catch that woke
A thousand raptured faces round
The dark and light befavoured ground.

They came and went; the tale is told —
How some were caught and some were bowled
And some had luck and half are laid
Under the fields where colours fade.

The pages turn until they near
The fatal doom-devoted year
When surlier umpires interposed
And War declared the innings closed.

Many the spinning coin, that bade
These fare a-field, those sit in shade,
Has called for ever from the sun
Into their last pavilion.

Enough; for here there lurks a ghost
Out-topping all the golden host,
A name at which I would not look.
Enough of dreaming. Close the book.

R. W. MOORE.

# SONGS

The beauty of the scene comes back to me as I write, comes to me as thoughts of a beloved countryside may stir in an exile's memories, or as a strain of music, perfect and exquisite, may possess the soul and ravish it anew.

A June evening in the Harrow meadows, the historic Hill with its spires twain silhouetted against the sky, and the gentle dusk has fallen and darkness is near at hand. A great concourse of acclaiming spectators beholds the pageanteers coming from out the dusk, coming from out the centuries and the wonderful yesterdays, coming with their costumes and colour. They assemble

in front of the grand stand, and a temple-hall
of Fame shines white through the dusk, and the
roll call of the greatest among Old Harrovians
is made; now Sir Robert Peel and now the Seventh
  Earl of Shaftesbury climb the temple stairs,
and now it is Sheridan and now Byron. The act
of Remembrance over, to a most solemn and
stately singing, the performers move slowly away
into the distance and the darkness.
'Tis Saturday evening and all the boys of Harrow School are present, and the aged Archbishop
of Canterbury is there, and he whispers to me,
moved by the sheer beauty and emotion of the
scene: "I might be in a cathedral, so beautiful
the singing and the setting"... And as their
spontaneous tribute, the boys themselves begin to
sing 'Forty Years On', and the welkin rings and
the stars come out as if to hearken...

SYDNEY WALTON. (1932)

93

I believe that my love for the school was made and fostered largely by these songs...they alone were concerned solely with beauty ~ beauty not perhaps of outward form, but beauty of character and ideal, of loyalty, love of friends and wonted place, and of a nameless understood chivalry...

One realised as in a flash of vision in darkness the meaning of life around one, its purpose and guiding unity. One knew oneself to be part of a tradition, greater than oneself, that gave meaning, beauty, and hope to all that one could do or endure.

ARTHUR BRYANT

# WHEN RALEIGH ROSE

EDWARD ERNEST BOWEN     1878     Music by JOHN FARMER

When Ra-leigh rose to fight the foes, We sprang to work and will; When Glo-ry gave to Drake the wave She gave to us the hill The a-ges drift in rolling tide But

94

high shall float the morn. A-down the stream of England's pride, When Drake and we were born! For we began when he began, Our times are one; His glory thus shall circle us Till time be done, till time be done, till time be done.

2. The Avon bears to endless years
    A magic voice along,
Where Shakespeare strayed in Stratford's shade,
    And waked the world to song.
We heard the music soft and wild,
    We thrilled to pulses new;
The winds that reared the Avon's child
    Were Herga's nurses too.
For we began when he began,
    Our times are one;
His glory thus shall circle us
    Till time be done...

# 'HERE SIR!'

E.W.HOWSON     1888     Music by EATON FANING

Here sir! Here sir! Here sir! Here sir! In the wind-y yard at Bill.

2. It is nought ~ our long procession,
   Father, brother, friend and son,
   As we step in quick succession,
   Cap and pass and hurry on?
   One and all
   At the call,
   Cap and pass and hurry on?
CHORUS:
   Here sir! Here sir! Here sir! Here sir!
   On the top of Harrow Hill
   Here sir! Here sir! Here sir! Here sir!
   In the windy yard at Bill.

3. One by one ~ and as they name us
   Forth we go from boyhood's rule,
   Sworn to be renown'd and famous
   For the honour of the School.
   True as steel, in our zeal,
   For the honour of the School.

CHORUS:

4. So today ~ and oh! if ever
   Duty's voice is ringing clear
   Bidding men to brave endeavour
   Be our answer "We are here!"
   Come what will
   Good or ill
   We will answer "We are here!"

CHORUS:

◄─◦◆◦◆◦►──

"I have always felt convinced that these songs must have played some part in Winston Churchill's subconscious mind when out of his transcendent courage, he compiled those wonderful speeches, so simple and so eternal in their youth and faith, in 1940."

ARTHUR BRYANT

97

# STET FORTUNA DOMUS

(Dedicated to Sir J. Savory, BART., M.P. Lord Mayor of London, 1891)

E. W. HOWSON  1891  Music by EATON FANING

Pray, charge your glass-es, gen-tle-men, And drink to Har-row's hon-our, May

Fortune still at-tend the Hill, And Glo-ry rest up-on her! The world out-side is

won-drous wide, But here the world is nar-row, One ma-gic thrall u-nites us all—The

name and fame of Har - row

3. Forgotten cheers are in our ears,
   Again we play our matches,
   And memory swells with wizard spells
   Our bygone scores and catches.
   Again we rush across the slush —
   A pack of breathless faces —
   And charge and fall, and see the ball
   Fly whizzing through the bases.

4. Tonight we praise the former days
   In patriotic chorus
   And celebrate the Good and Great
   Who trod the Hill before us;
   Where Sheridan and Peel began,
   And Temple's frame of iron
   Where Ashley vow'd to serve the Crowd
   And song awoke in Byron.

5. So once again your glasses drain,
   And may we long continue
   From Harrow School to rise and rule
   By heart and brain and sinew.
   And as the roll of Honour's Scroll
   Page after page is written,
   May Harrow give the names that live
   In Great and Greater Britain!

The following verse was written for the visit of Mr.
Winston Churchill on 18th December, 1940 by Edward
Plumptre.

Nor less we praise in _darker_ days
The leader of our nation,
And CHURCHILL'S name shall win acclaim
From each new generation.
While in this fight to guard the Right
Our country you defend, Sir,
Here grim and gay we mean to stay,
And stick it to the end, Sir.

This was the beginning of a tradition, for year after
year, throughout the war and until 1961, Churchill

99

was to climb the Hill and join his old School in singing Harrow songs – "those songs I knew so well and loved so much."

"They are a great treasure and possession of Harrow School and keep the flame burning in a marvellous manner. Many carry them with them all their lives... They are wonderful; marvellous; more than could be put into bricks and mortar, or treasured in any trophies of silver or gold..."

In 1941, after the Songs, Churchill addressed the School:
"Almost a year has passed since I came down here at your Headmaster's kind invitation in order to cheer myself.....by singing some of our own songs. The ten months that have passed have seen very terrible catastrophic events in the world – ups and downs, misfortunes – but can anyone here this afternoon not feel deeply thankful for what has happened in the time that has passed and for the very great improvement in the position of our country and of our home? Why, when I was here last time, we were quite alone, desperately alone.....we had the unmeasured menace of the enemy and their air attack still beating upon us. But for everyone, surely, what we have gone through in this period – I am addressing myself to the School – surely from this period of ten months, this is the lesson: never give in, never give in, never;

100

never, never, never ~ in nothing, great or small, large or petty ~ never give in except to convictions of honour and good sense. Never yield to force; never yield to the apparently overwhelming might of the enemy. We stood all alone a year ago, and to many countries it seemed that our account was closed, we were finished. All this tradition of ours, our songs, our School history, which is so much a part of the history of this country, were gone and finished and liquidated."

"Very different is the mood today. Britain, other nations thought, had drawn a sponge across her slate. But instead, our country stood in the gap. There was no flinching and no thought of giving in ... "

"You sang here a verse of a School song; you sang that extra verse written in my honour, but there is one word in it I want to alter. It is the line:

'Nor less we praise in darker days'.

I have obtained the Head Master's permission to alter 'darker' to 'sterner'. Do not let us speak of 'darker days', let us speak rather of 'sterner days' These are not dark days: these are great days ~ the greatest days our country has ever lived ~ and we must all thank God that we have been allowed, each of us according to our stations, to play a part in making these days memorable in the history of our race".

# FORTY YEARS ON

EDWARD ERNEST BOWEN      1872      Music by JOHN FARMER

For-ty years on when a-far and a-sunder Parted are those who are singing today

When you look back, and for-get-fully wonder What you were like in your work and your play

Then, it may be, there will often come o'er you, Glimpses of notes like the catch of a song~

Visions of boyhood shall float them before you. Echoes of dreamland shall bear them along. Follow

CHORUS

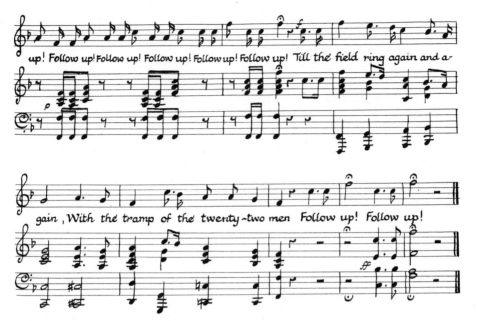

up! Follow up! Follow up! Follow up! Follow up! Follow up! Till the field ring again and a-

gain, With the tramp of the twenty-two men Follow up! Follow up!

3. O the great days, in the distance enchanted,
   Days of fresh air, in the rain and the sun,
   How we rejoiced as we struggled and panted,
   Hardly believable, forty years on!
   How we discoursed of them, one with another,
   Auguring triumph, or balancing fate,
   Loved the ally with the heart of a brother
   Hated the foe with a playing at hate!

4. Forty years on, growing older and older,
   Shorter in wind, as in memory long,
   Feeble of foot, and rheumatic of shoulder,
   What will it help you that once you were strong?
   God give us bases to guard or beleaguer,
   Games to play out, whether earnest or fun;
   Fights for the fearless, and goals for the eager,
   Twenty and thirty and forty years on.

And when we quit our boyhood's happy scene,
And a new race shall live and learn, may they
Prove better, nobler-souled than we have been.
Where'er we rove on life's all-varied way,
May the fond image of the loved Hill stay
To soothe our trials, and our triumphs share.

WALTER SYDNEY SICHEL

103

# FAREWELL

Harrovians, I regret to see you go,
Like energies drained from the body,
Leaving it mute and still.
Will you remember the essence –
Essential frame of law,
Or will the lesser aspects call?
Stone wall, wed to sun, embossed with lion;
Low fields carpeting, call of bell;
Blend of impressions.
Or impassioned hours;
The gordian knots of friend and foe,
But in reality all friend.
The moving tides wash through the day,
A measured pulse observed;
Boater and bluer seen
As a sameness, but within, diversity.
With time, the manhood mark is traced,
The fires temper, the form is given.
An instrument for life.

DOROTHY BOUX

104

Yet the time may come,
            though you scarce know why,
When your eyes will fill
            at the thought of the Hill,
And the wild regret
            of the last goodbye.


'Five Hundred Faces'
            E.W. HOWSON   1883.

## THE HILL ~ NOW

Did they grow here, these buildings?
Did they spring up from rock and root?
So well-matched, well-married
To the curving undulation of the Hill ~
Voluptuous breast of earth
Nurturing fine-boned arch,
Sturdy column; limbs of step and stone
Honed by the rub and run of feet,
Ten thousand feet or more ~
Like great sea-tides washed over
A smooth, receptive shore.

Were these boys always here'?
Did they spring up from rock and root?
So strong-built, well-tuned
To the fair and firm tradition of the Hill.
They were always here', these boys ~
The life of the stone'-born limb,
Honed by the ancient law
And ruled by a thousand words or more',
Like great sea-tides washed over
A muttering, moving shore'.

DOROTHY BOUX

# HARROW ON THE HILL

When melancholy Autumn comes to Wembley
And electric trains are lighted after tea
The poplars near the Stadium are trembly
With their tap and tap and whispering to me,
Like the sound of little breakers
Spreading out along the surf-line
When the estuary's filling with the sea.

Then Harrow on the Hill's a rocky island
And Harrow churchyard full of sailors' graves
And the constant click and kissing of the trolley-
                              buses hissing
Is the level to the Wealdstone turned to waves.
And the rumble of the railway
Is the thunder of the rollers
As they gather up for plunging into caves.

There's a storm cloud to the westward over Kenton,
There's a line of harbour lights at Perivale,
Is it rounding rough Pentire in a flood of sunset
                                    fire

The little fleet of trawlers under sail?
Can those boats be only roof tops
As they steam along the skyline
In a race for port and Padstow with the gale?


JOHN BETJEMAN

( A few late Chrysanthemums - 1954 )


...I think of dusk in Grove Wood, alone with a trench where
we had sought to unravel some of the mysteries of the Past
that lay hidden in the ground. And the Spirits of the Wood,
that had guarded the place since it was a sacred Saxon
Grove, seemed to stir around me and urge me to leave un-
touched their dark secrets.
They allowed me to find a seven-hundred-year-old sherd
of pottery, a tantalising flint scraper and a slumbering earth-
work, and then they closed up their book and revealed no
more. In my dreams I still search for the early Temple
on the Hill: but its Guardians preserve it from our pry-
ing eyes. And perhaps that is how it should be.

J. S. GOLLAND

# MEMORIES

Almost a hundred years ago, the Harrow Historian Percy
Thornton wrote about the School Custos of his time "...his
mind is a repository of Harrow experience...and history"
How well those words could apply to Custos Wilkinson,
present custodian of Harrow School.

"One of my earliest memories is the Harrow Historical Pageant
when, as a boy, I played under the wooden stage...
We have had all sorts of pranks from the boys! I remember one
boy who tied a huge bow-tie to the top of the church steeple and
a steeplejack had to get it down.
We have had our local characters too. There was an old man who
lived in a lodging house in Crown Street, early this century, called
Mr. Ambridge. He lived from the boys in his latter years. They
would lower bottles down from their windows on a piece of string
and he got them filled at the local public-houses so the boys nick-
named him "Bottles". Once a year the boys kitted him out in topper
and tails and took him to Lord's; then he used to wear the outfit
for the rest of the year.
Then there was an old organ-grinder who lived in Sudbury. Once
a week, he would bring his donkey and barrel organ up the Hill
and play it in the High Street.
The School is a great institution with its comradeship, and a
way of life which leads to an understanding of people.
The boys deserve a lot because they sacrifice a lot. They

give up a home life and because of this a great understanding
develops in them, and strength of character.
They learn discipline and hard work. From the start they must
work or they cannot stay. This training sticks to them
for the rest of their lives. They will never give up easily.
They are not allowed to give in.
When I look back I think what a wonderful thing that this
School exists. Disciplined boys can accept knocks better in later
life ~ they can take knocks and give knocks if it is required.

I shall miss this life when I retire; the company of the boys
and the local people, the Hill . . ."

S. G. WILKINSON

'BOTTLES'

# Mr. Trundle Remembers...

(For generations of Harrow boys, Mr. Trundle has epitomised
Gieves, one of the School outfitters on the Hill, where
he came in 1936.)

Before the 1939/45 War, "Lords" was a very special occasion
in the Harrow School Calendar, and particularly as far as
"Dress" was concerned.

In those days, all boys wore Toppers, and to ensure that these
were looking good, arrangements were made for a man from
the Hatmaker's to visit the School shop, where he ironed and
polished hats for two complete days.

Small boys wore their Eton suits, but a white waistcoat re-
placed the usual black one for this day. Instead of the Harrow
tailcoat, boys were expected to wear a morning coat, with a
grey waistcoat and grey morning trousers. The majority of
boys would have black ebony canes, with the Harrow blue
tassel attached, and their buttonholes displaying the blue corn-
flower.

All this created enthusiasm for the social gathering, as well
as for the match itself. Normally, whichever side won, "hat
bashing" took place. Consequently there was considerable
demand for new Toppers to be made in time for the next
Sunday.

I look back upon that time with nostalgia, tinged with regret, knowing that such days are gone for ever.

1980

# LUNCH AT HARROW

For Thursday's Child it was the most natural thing in the world of superstition that, after a New York childhood and adolescence, I should settle in Harrow as a Housemaster's wife. Such things happen every day! But, what a surprise to find in 1967, six hundred feet above sea-level and thirty minutes from Piccadilly, a community of people who wore strange clothes and hats and CAME HOME TO LUNCH! You may find this hard to believe, but at noon a hush descended over the Hill, shops drew their blinds and locked their doors and, for an hour or more, people of all ages sat down together to eat and talk. The rest of the day was spent in post-prandial torpor: bad for work, but good for the soul. Every day was a bit like Sunday.

Coming home to lunch to be reunited with one's family only a few hours after breakfast was a great luxury for husbands and children and for those bachelors who were favourite uncles at these feasts. My foreign city-bred eyes detected in this custom many signs of the 'civilised' atmosphere of earlier, palmier English days: leisure, the art of conversation, dining rooms (Harrow abounds with large dining rooms and tables still), children, cats and dogs curled up in the corner, a servant perhaps (one family employed a special lunch cook), fires, wine, laughter and steamed pudding.

In the Grove dining hall (each of the eleven Houses dined 'at home') Harry Phillips, the butler, dressed in full fig, served seventy boys individually, correcting their sloppy manners with the ironic rebuke

"Mind your manners, my Lord ~ you're not at home now
you know!"

Behind all this was an army of unsung heroines: the wives, matrons, cooks and au pairs who, every day, managed and planned and shopped and cooked and served and cleared these splendid meals.

In the 1970s, all this began to change, and finally, in 1977, the Shepherd-Churchill Room was opened so that all 750 boys and any masters who so wished could dine together. The house servants retired or were re-employed, some by the new dining hall. A bad day for 'civilisation' perhaps, but a great day for women?

MELISA TREASURE

---

## HOUSE PLAY CONFUSIONS

Bright lights, smell of greasepaint,
Chaos backstage ~ what's to be done?
Nerves tingle, the "lead" feels faint,
Props broken, cues lost and won.

Actors look at each other, "Here we go" ~
Are all the audience there? Hang on ~ NO!
The players strut their fretful hour with great success;
Tomorrow and tomorrow ~ clearing up the mess!

JOHN GORE

# SHAKESPEARE ON THE HILL

There had been performances of Shakespeare at Harrow School before 1940, but in that year an accident occurred which may be called the first cause of the present series of Shakespearian productions on the Hill. One night in October, an incendiary bomb lodged in the roof of Speech Room. Fire and water, by destroying the mechanism for suspending a proscenium curtain, and the wiring needed for floodlight and spotlight, confronted would-be Harrovian actors with something like the primitive conditions of the Elizabethan playhouse.

'There is some soul of goodness in things evil,
Would men observingly distil it out.'

In the summer of 1941 TWELFTH NIGHT was produced in these conditions. The actors played before a neutral curtain-background, with an occasional inset disclosed by parting the back-curtain. When they stood on the central steps or in the well, they had their audience all round them, in intimate contact. The stage was "unlocalised", taking its momentary geography from the characters who walked on it, or from the hints given ~ when he wanted to define it ~ by the Poet himself; a barrel of beer rolled on to the platform helped the imagination to descend into the cellar, boxtrees in the inset furnished forth Olivia's garden. The light was daylight throughout, with a candle to give verisimilitude to Sir Toby's contention that "not to be a-bed after midnight is to be up betimes." Music was used only where Shakespeare demanded it, and for Shakespeare's explicit dramatic purpose. The women s' parts, as in Shakespeare's time, were played by boys.

In 1942 the mood of the nation had changed, and Shakespeare's Elizabethan Epic seemed in season. HENRY THE FIFTH was moreover a challenge to test still further the creed that the plays are best performed in the kind of theatre they were written for. An actor dressed as Shakespeare himself spoke his choruses and expounded his method: "Let us ... on your imaginary forces work ... Piece out our imperfections with your thoughts ... Think when we talk of horses that you see them ...'tis your thoughts that now must deck our kings ... Work, work your thoughts, and therein see a siege ..." We learnt then that the spoken word which Shakespeare gave his actors to speak could create darkness

115

in the steady "daylight": it became, and has been ever since, an element of our reconstruction of the Poet's method that the steady light in Speech Room remains the same throughout the evening's performance. The night before the battle of Agincourt was especially gripping. Every eye in Speech Room was peering through the shadows in fear of the Frenchmen, overwhelming in their numbers: the Poet's apology for the resources of his stage seemed needless: his audience were in camp, at midnight before the day of battle, and felt genuine comfort when they heard the hushed voice of their commander:

> Gloucester, 'tis true that we are in great danger;
> The greater therefore should our courage be.

The year was 1942, and before the war was over, there were precious friends hid in death's dateless night: among those killed in action were King Henry himself, Ancient Pistol, Malvolio, and Orsino. The boastful Dolphin of France became the modest hero of a famous naval engagement.

A comedy, a history ~ inevitably the third year of the series was to see a tragedy. MACBETH offered at once the most formidable challenge and the most tantalising opportunity; by this test the Poet's method must stand or fall. Here was a story which must be imagined to take place not only for the most part in natural darkness, but ever and anon with supernatural horror hovering in the fog and filthy air. There was always the comforting assurance that Shakespeare himself had devised the play for the conditions of his own theatre: it remained but to infer or guess how he and his fellow-actors had solved each problem at their first performance.

One of Banquo's murderers at rehearsal was uncomfortable about the poetical style of his lines:

> The west yet glimmers with some streaks of day:
> Now spurs the lated traveller apace
> To gain the timely inn.

He was told that his task ~ the task Shakespeare had given him- was to bring down upon the "daylit" stage the dusk in which his victim was to be murdered. The actor was appalled to hear that he had to play the scene by daylight: "I couldn't do it in daylight: it wouldn't seem natural." Don't worry, he was told, you were in the audience last year; you remember the scene of the night before Agincourt? It will be just like that. "Oh yes," he said, "but then it <u>was</u> dark." He remembered the scene as taking place in the dark. It was a turning point in our history: we have never doubted Shakespeare's power of illusion since.

Year by year new features of Shakespeare's Wooden O were incorporated in the wooden D of Speech Room. The whole of the well was boarded over to make a stage as spacious as that of the Globe, jutting out into the midst of the audience, so that contact was at arm's length. Then on scaffolding was built the façade of the Tiring~House, with its curtained discovery~space, and its stage "above". Window~stages were a further development, to give occasional locality to the great Doors at either end of the Tiring~House. The dressing of the stage has been no more elaborate than the furniture and properties necessary for the action of the play: Peter Quince, in A MIDSUMMER NIGHT'S DREAM, drew up a bill of properties "such as our play wants": a moss~bank (familiar item from the property store) has done duty for the slumbers of Titania, for the Player King, for Lorenzo and Jessica "in such a night". The Music, as always with Shakespeare, has been an integral part of the plays, heard by and commented on by those on stage, and in period not later than the closing of Shakespeare's playhouse in 1642. The Costumes likewise have not strayed in fashion beyond that date. Music or costume of a later period will introduce moods and fashions which were beyond Shakespeare's experience ~ because he was dead. The infinite variety of his imagination needs no embellishment from later ages.

As the physical features in Speech Room came year by year to approximate more nearly to those of the Globe playhouse, so the conditions of performance grew closer to Shakespeare's own. And in these conditions we found that it was by <u>the spoken word</u> of our actors that the playhouse came to life. We learnt each year how immensely powerful were Shakespeare's words to create illusion ~ of action, of atmosphere, of place, of character, of mood, of reaction.

Over the years there have been many notable performances. Prince Hal won the commendation of the wisest of dramatic critics; Helena was remembered years afterwards in California; Cleopatra astonished the Poet Laureate on his first visit to the Harrow Globe; King Lear persuaded one spectator that

117

the lights were turned to blue during the storm scenes of the third Act; Hamlet's princely intelligence raised a smile of assent from the Principal of a famous Drama School when he asked "Do the boys carry it away?" and received the answer "Ay, that they do, my lord; Hercules and his load too."

There have been other happy coincidences, arising (for instance) out of the geography of the Hill itself. Feste being questioned by Viola: "Dost thou live by thy tabor?" "No sir, I live by the church." "Art thou a churchman?" "No such matter, sir: I do live by the church; for I do live at my house, and my house doth stand by the church." A glance in the direction of St. Mary's added point to the dialogue. Or the Spaniard Armado asking Holofernes the schoolmaster: "Do you not educate youth at the charge-house on the mountain?" and Holofernes's pedantic reply; "Or <u>mons</u>, the hill," inevitably raised in the mind's eye of the audience a vision of the Fourth Form Room, where John Lyon's first beneficiaries were taught their hornbook. Over the years too, since 1941, the Harrow Globe has accumulated its legends ~ as of Hamlet's father's Ghost (a part which Shakespeare himself played) filling in the long gap between his first and later appearances by haunting wayfarers between the tombstones of St. Mary's churchyard.

No less than twenty-four plays of the canon have been performed in this Harrow Globe ~ some of them more than once, A MIDSUMMER NIGHT'S DREAM in a by now traditional production, based on the obligatory question "What did the Chamberlain's Men do?". The strongest proof of the strength of such a tradition is to be seen in the formation of the Old Harrovian Players' Company in 1952. The members of this company, whose ages range from eighteen to fifty or more, rehearse a play each year (they have not missed a year since their foundation) during the Spring holiday, meeting for the most part at week-ends, and in conditions of improvisation which suggest the regular practice of the Chamberlain's Men themselves. So deeply ingrained in the nature of these actors is the Poet's Method which they have learnt in their years at school that their performances, though less meticulously rehearsed than those of the School, are yet wholly to be enjoyed as a faithful representation of the Poet's intention.

Historians of this tradition will find some interesting lines of development ~ Queen Elinor who became old Adam who

118

rose to King Lear; Costard to Shylock; Ophelia to Cardinal Pandulph. The continuity is indeed remarkable, and in the course of forty years there has grown up a company spirit that can justly claim kinship with the Lord Chamberlain's/King James's Men of the Poet's lifetime. One actor holds a record of having trodden the boards of the Harrow Globe stage every year for thirty years; he may well be named Harrow's Richard Burbage, for he has played almost all the Shakespearian roles which Burbage made famous. Another has shown the versatility and power of Thomas Pope, counting Antony , Hotspur, Kent, Lear, Othello, Iago Costard, Jaques and Dogberry among his many successes. A third veteran of the company graduated as Viola and Hippolyta, and has since been Petruchio, Glendower, Prospero, Malvolio, Justice Shallow, Don Armado, Macbeth, Iago . . . Like their predecessors in 1600, they have been willing also to eke out the company's performance by playing three-line or speechless characters, when need was. It is a harmonious company, singularly free from envy and grudge and self-importance ~ as one may guess for the most part Shakespeare's own company was, "without ambition either of self~profit, or fame: only to keep the memory of so worthy a friend, and fellow alive, as was our Shakespeare."

Now it is possible for any boy during his four years at Harrow School to witness eight plays of Shakespeare performed in the conditions for which he wrote. And in this year 1981 the Harrow Globe can at last claim to have reached forty years on.

RONALD WATKINS

# SHERIDAN AND HARROW

**H**arrow plays a significant part in the story of Richard Brinsley Sheridan (1751–1816), Whig politician, playwright and manager of Drury Lane Theatre. He first came to the Hill in 1762 as an eleven-year-old schoolboy. "As he may probably fall into a bustling life", wrote his mother, "we have a mind to accustom him to shift for himself." But shifting for himself at boarding school filled the boy with an appalling sense of isolation, and this must have intensified when, in 1764, his father Thomas "bid defiance to his merciless creditors" by spiriting the rest of the family off to France. Thomas Sheridan was an actor and Richard had to undergo the gibes of superior Harrovians as a poor player's son. On at least one occasion he gave as good as he got. To a doctor's son who scoffed at Thomas Sheridan's profession, he riposted, "'Tis true, my father lives by pleasing people; but yours lives by killing them."

**F**orty years on, Sheridan told a friend that at Harrow "he was a very low-spirited boy, much given to crying when alone, and he attributed this. . . to his being left without money, and not often taken home at the regular holidays." However, during his last two years there, things looked up for him. Samuel Parr, his senior by a mere four years, came back to his old school to teach, spotted young Sheridan's potential and took a personal interest in him. Many years later Lord Holland heard Sheridan "relate with tears in his eyes, that he never met with kindness at school but from Dr. Parr".

**R**ichard left Harrow around 1767~8 and his progress through the subsequent decade is famous in the annals of romantic and

120

theatrical history. In a sensational courtship which involved an elopement and two duels, he wooed and won the lovely and wildly-adored singer, Elizabeth Linley, the most promising soprano of her day. Next he wrote a comedy, "THE RIVALS", and an opera, "THE DUENNA; he succeeded David Garrick as the proprietor of Drury Lane; and there he set the capstone on his dramatic reputation with "THE SCHOOL FOR SCANDAL".

But then, abruptly, with the production of THE CRITIC in 1779, his creative contribution to the theatre was effectively at an end. This play, according to Lord Byron, the best of all farces, persistently concerns itself not only with the theatre, its major theme, but with politics too. And it is likely that Sheridan had been impelled to buy Drury Lane less by an ardent love of the drama than by the wish to finance his political career out of the proceeds. For some time now he had been dabbling in political journalism, his literary celebrity had brought him into contact with many of the leading Whigs of the time, and he finally committed himself to the world of politics when, at the general election of 1780, he was voted into Parliament by the "free and independent electors of Stafford". It was, he said, the happiest moment of his life. He remained in Parliament for more than three decades, and politics, not the theatre, proved his most intense and durable passion.

The following year, Richard and his wife Elizabeth took a long lease on The Grove on Harrow Hill ~ "a very pretty place," enthused Elizabeth. The fine Georgian house still stands, as do its stables, now converted into form rooms frequented by latter-day Harrovians. The couple had moved here with the intention of sending their son Tom to his father's old school. But ten years previously, when the Governors of Harrow passed over Samuel Parr, Richard's mentor, as Head Master, highly dramatic ructions involving a riot among the boys occurred, and Parr shook the dust of the Hill from his feet. He was now running a small educational establishment at Hatton in Warwickshire and the Sheridans, no doubt from feelings of loyalty towards him, thought it best to send Tom there. However, Elizabeth's youngest brother, William Linley, was a boy at Harrow between 1780 and 1785 and looked back on these times when he wrote in 1825 to an early biographer of Sheridan who had recorded some of the practical jokes so characteristic of him:

"I suspect," says Linley, "that the Gambols you have noticed were played principally at Harrow. One farce I well remember, being myself a spectator of these, for I was at school at the time and lived with S and my sister. Fitzpatrick, Tickell and my sister Mrs. Tickell were of the party. The gentlemen had been left as usual by the ladies after dinner and when summoned to Coffee, found, on entering the room, not the

Ladies, but several Barristers in their gowns and wigs, in high debate with parchments before them, a huge bowl of punch, pipes, and tobacco. The rest of the fun was to discover each lady ~ they were all variously and ludicrously masked ~ according to her gesture and disguised tone of voice . . ."

The Fitzpatrick here referred to was a fellow Member of Parliament while Richard Tickell was Sheridan's closest friend, a littérateur whose pen was ever at the disposal of the Whig party. It was in fact Whig politicians rather than any literary set that came to see the Sheridans at Harrow; indeed, according to Lord Thanet, Sheridan "at no part of his life liked any allusion to his being a dramatic author". We have a delightful glimpse of Edmund Burke wheeling young Tom Sheridan "rapidly" in a child's hand chaise on the Hill; and Charles James Fox was a frequent visitor. This proved a time of feverish political activity for Sheridan who took up office in 1782 as Under-Secretary of State for the Northern Department and then served as a secretary to the Treasury in the discreditable Fox/North Ministry of 1783. With Richard up in town, Elizabeth must have often lamented her Harrow solitude. "Situated as I am at present," she grieved in one letter, " I know nothing of anybody or anything". But she found comfort in the Grove garden where, according to tradition, her favourite spot looked out towards Windsor.

Sheridan changed residences with a compulsive frequency and by February 1784 he had left Harrow and established himself in Bruton Street in London. His defection was confirmed when he sent his son by a second marriage to Winchester. Yet Harrow came to regard him with great esteem. "Don't forget," wrote Lord Byron, "that he was at school at Harrow, where in my time (1801~1805), we used to show his name ~ R.B. Sheridan, 1765 ~ as an honour to the walls." This carving, one of the many dug deep into the Jacobean panelling, is still pointed out to visitors in the school's Fourth Form Room.

JAMES MORWOOD

# BYRON THE HARROVIAN

Seat of my youth! thy distant spire
Recalls each scene of joy;
My bosom glows with former fire, —
In mind again a boy.
Thy grove of elms, thy verdant hill,
Thy every path delights me still . . .

(L'Amitié Est l'Amour Sans Ailes, 1806)

In 1801 Edward Long, a new boy at Harrow, wrote to his father, "There is another . . . a lame fellow just come, he seems a good sort of fellow." George Gordon, sixth Lord Byron, born in London with a club foot on January 22nd, 1788, lost his father when only three, and was brought up by his mother in Scotland. While at Aberdeen Grammar School in 1798 he inherited the barony from his great-uncle, of Newstead Abbey, Nottinghamshire. Moving with his mother to Nottingham, Byron entered Dr. Glennie's school at Dulwich. In April 1801 John Hanson, the family solicitor, brought him to Harrow.

The Rev. Joseph Drury had been Master since 1785, a period of prosperity for the School. He wrote, "I soon found that a wild mountain colt had been submitted to my management." He assigned to Byron his son Henry as tutor. Byron later granted that Dr. Drury was "the best . . . friend I ever had".

Byron hated Harrow at first. He was bullied, and admitted, "I was a most unpopular boy." But he was no coward. "I fought my way very fairly. I think I lost but one battle out of seven." By the end of June Dr. Drury had placed him in the Fourth Form. He spent the summer with the Hansons and his mother, in London and Cheltenham. Back at Harrow, he eagerly joined in everything. He would gain renown as a swimmer, boxer, fencer and cricketer. He spent Christmas with his mother in London, returning to School in February 1802.

Byron read very widely. "I was never seen reading, but always idle and in mischief, or at play. The truth is that I . . . read when no one else reads." Thus "I was . . . remarked for the extent and readiness of my general information."

Mrs. Byron returned for the Easter or summer holiday from Bath to London; Byron rode in Hyde Park with Major Pryse Gordon, who wrote, "He was a fine, lively, restless lad, full of fire and energy." That autumn William Harness entered the School, also lame. Byron said: "If any fellow bullies you, I'll thrash him if I can." They became friends; Byron confessed later, "The first lines I ever attempted at Harrow were addressed to you." Byron often stole away to the churchyard, musing for hours beneath an elm tree on the Peachey tomb.

'Barry Cornwall' wrote of Byron the poet: "There were . . . no symptoms of such a destiny. He was loud, even coarse . . . a rough, curly-headed boy, and apparently nothing more." Byron observed of Dr. Drury, too: "My first Harrow verses . . . were received by him but coolly. No one had the least notion that I should subside into poesy." Just then, indeed, Henry Drury complained about Byron's "inattention to business and . . . propensity to make others laugh". Back in Bath for Christmas, Byron claimed that Henry Drury had "used me ill for some time past". Dr. Drury agreed to transfer Byron to Mr. Evans' house.

During 1803 Byron's friendships developed. "P. Hunter, Curzon, Long and Tattersall were my principal friends." Edward Noel Long, 'Cleon' in Byron's lengthy 'Childish Recollections', "was a less boisterous spirit than mine. I was always cricketing, rebelling, fighting . . . while he was more sedate." John Cecil Tattersall ('Davus') saved Byron from being clubbed with a musket during a fight with rustics. Another friend, George Sinclair, "the prodigy of our School days . . . made exercises for half the School."

Byron also led a younger circle, especially in 1804-5. "Clare, Dorset, Chas. Gordon, De Bath(e), Claridge and Jno. Wingfield, were my juniors and favourites, whom I spoilt by indulgence." John, Earl of Clare ('Lycus'), was eleven in 1803; George, Duke of Dorset, would be Byron's fag and feature in several poems; and the Hon. John Wingfield ('Alonzo') would also be his fag and be elegised in 'Childe Harold's Pilgrimage.'

Of the above Byron wrote: "My School friendships were with me passions. . . That with Lord Clare began one of the earliest and lasted longest." In February 1803 a quarrel with George John, Earl Delawarr ('Euryalus'), inspired Byron's earliest existing Harrow poem.

After Easter 1803 Byron wrote that Henry Drury "behaved himself in a manner I neither can nor will bear." Dr. Drury apologised for his son, telling Hanson that Byron "possesses. . . a mind that feels". He informed Lord Carlisle, Byron's guardian, that the young lord had "talents. . . which will add lustre to his rank". So in June Byron wrote: "I have been placed in a higher form today, and Dr. Drury and I go on very well."

Mrs. Byron had moved to Southwell, but Byron spent his holiday at Newstead, falling "distractedly" but vainly in love with Mary Chaworth of Annesley. He was so unhappy that his mother let him stay away from School until January 1804. He now corresponded with his half~sister, the Hon. Augusta Byron, telling her: "I do not dislike Harrow; I find ways and means to amuse myself very pleasantly there."

This "clever, plain-spoken and undaunted boy" sometimes expressed daring opinions. Defending his Napoleon statue against the "time"~servers", he fought Lord Calthorpe for writing "Damned atheist" under his name. That summer Dr. Drury accused him of making "a scene of riot and confusion." Byron also complained to his mother that Mark Drury, the Master's brother, was "continually reproaching me with the narrowness of my fortune . . . But. . . the way to riches, to greatness lies before me. . . I will carve myself the passage to grandeur, but never with dishonour." Later that term, indeed, the Master praised Byron's declamation at a Speech Day rehearsal. "Dr. Drury had a great notion that I should turn out an orator." He did well on the day, playing Latinus in a dialogue from the Aeneid. Robert Peel also spoke. Byron recalled: "As a declaimer and actor I was reckoned at least his equal; . . . in School, he always knew his lesson, and I rarely."

Mrs. Byron was then writing: "He is truly amiable and . . . writes a great deal of poetry." But at Southwell that summer Byron quarrelled with his irascible mother, admitting afterwards, "I am rather too fidgety." His letters to Augusta during the autumn show a widening rift with his mother: "She is so. . . impatient, that I dread the approach of the holidays." He was consoled by Augusta's friendship. "If you too desert me, I have nobody I can love but Delawarr. . . the most good-tempered, amiable, clever fellow."

Relations with Dr. Drury fluctuated. Byron told Augusta: "This. . .

morning I had a thundering Jobation from our good Doctor, which deranged my nervous system . . . But . . . I cannot help liking him and will remember his instructions with gratitude." At Christmas, however, Dr. Drury, due to retire at Easter 1805, wrote that Byron's "conduct gave me much trouble and uneasiness," he recommended that Byron should leave. Hanson, who put Byron up over Christmas, pleaded that not returning would "amount . . . to an expulsion." So in February 1805 Byron went back to School.

There were three candidates for the Mastership: Mark Drury, Benjamin Evans and Dr. George Butler of Sidney Sussex College, Cambridge. Byron's fellow-monitor Tom Wildman yielded Byron leadership of a faction supporting Drury.

Byron spent his Easter holiday between London and Southwell. Returning for his last term, "I so much disliked leaving Harrow that . . . it broke my very rest." Dr. Butler had been appointed Master. In contrast to Dr. Drury ('Probus'), Byron satirised him as 'Pomposus', attacking his "narrow brain", "new fangled rules" and "vain parade". Dr. Butler maintained dignified silence; Byron would ultimately be reconciled with him.

Now the third boy in the School, Byron swam, cricketed and caroused at Mother Barnard's. On the Speech Day of June 6th he triumphed with Zanga's tirade over Alonzo's body, from Young's 'The Revenge.' He invited Augusta to attend the second Speech Day on July 4th "in one of his Lordship's most dashing carriages", and put great effort into declaiming King Lear's harangue to the storm.

His final day came. Young Henry Long saw him descend after carving his name on the boards. Above the fighting-ground Byron said: "That is the spot where I hope your blood will often be shed."

On August 2nd Byron played in the first cricket match against Eton, writing to Charles Gordon: "We . . . were most confoundedly beat . . . After the match we dined . . . and went . . . to the Haymarket Theatre, where we kicked up a row."

In 1817 Byron declared: "I believe no one could . . . be more attached to Harrow than I have always been." He was brought up without father or brothers, and "friendship will be doubly dear ~To one who thus for kindred hearts must roam, ~And seek abroad the love denied at home. ~Those hearts, dear Ida [Harrow], have I found in thee, ~A home a world, a paradise to me." (Childish Recollections, 1806)

MICHAEL REES

# THE PILGRIM OF ETERNITY

In Memoriam   —   19th April 1824.

Thy fame, now mostly clouded, still shines clear
On the fair Hill where thou were wont to woo
Beneath yon ancient elms the spirit who
Haunts Helicon, and whispered in thy ear
Of days when thou wouldst thrill a hemisphere...

Afar thou didst depart,
And fired with the resolve to liberate
The ruined realm of Poesy and Art
From tyranny's thrall, didst nobly meet thy fate.

William Toynbee

In 1941, on the occasion of the anniversary of the Greek Day of Independence, the Head Master, at the request of the Monitors, sent the following message to the King of the Hellenes.
"From the Hill where Byron went to School, we, the present members of Harrow, watch your heroic defence of that freedom for which he died: and we beg to offer your Majesty and the people of Greece this expression of our admiration, our homage and our unshaken belief in the justice of our common cause."
The following reply was received.
"...at Harrow, where Byron received his introduction to Greek culture, one of the first links in the chain uniting Modern Greece and Great Britain was forged; that the feelings of those who inhabit the same Hill to-day should after more than a century remain unchanged makes this document memorable as a striking example of British constancy.
On December 17th 1942 the King visited the School. He was officially welcomed by the Head Master and in modern Greek by Lawrence J. Verney.

ΜΕΓΑΛΕΙΟΤΑΤΕ!
ὀχι μόνον προνομιοῦχον καὶ τιμητικὸν...

It is not only a privilege and an honour to welcome the King of the Hellenes to Harrow, but we are also given an opportunity of expressing to Your Majesty, and thus to the whole people of Greece, our admiration and respect for the unrivalled and imperishable bravery with which they fought and are fighting for their country.
He was once a boy in this School who on the plain of Missolonghi lit the torch of freedom: so also was our Prime Minister, who most assuredly will again establish the freedom of Greece after this long night.
In the name of the boys of Harrow School I welcome your Majesty, and it is with the utmost sincerity I say

ΖΗΤΩ Η ΕΛΛΑΣ

Long live Greece!

127

# November Morning on the Hill

*It is, perhaps, strange*
*that in the guide book the visitor*
*finds no mention of any reaction,*
*no spark or sizzle*
*as the tear-drop*
*(of laughter ?)*
*stoops to the churned clay.*
*The oaks moult in the fleecy mist*
*and the elms would have continued*
*to be immemorial,*

*yet, whilst an island's smallest events*
*find documentation, and historians*
*harrow their steaming, private hells,*
*(for there is terror*
*in the unnoticed rhythms*
*of traffic),*
*obscurity covers that vital moment*
*of impact. The sweat of the rugger match*
*swells the subterranean waters*
*which give life*

*to the hill's sacred trees,*
*erode still further the drenched,*
*dazzled and annotated monuments*
*and, above all,*
*lubricate the ants' nest*
*of emotions.*
*See, they return! Yes, we return,*
*for when, as old as those*
*who governed our youth, we realise*
*that our being*

*lies wholly in the grit,*
*the mud, and under the lawns*
*and gardens that passively accepted*
*the brief swarming*
*and silent knowledge*
    *of expectancy,*
*we — human — have no option*
*but to lead our memories to drink*
*of the bewilderment, hatred, friendship,*
    *leading to*

*Pride, that we met on this rise*
*above the seething undergrowth*
*of brick. It is here*
*that our sentimentality fades*
*to a composite oblivion*
    *of landscape.*
*Here, in a tradition, we prepared*
*for life, while unwittingly we lived it.*
*It is perhaps strange that we*
    *never knew death.*

     D. A. HERLING
    A young poet at Harrow, 1980

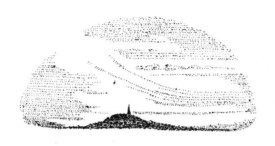

## THE GATES OF DAWN

Over the plain of night there brooded a vast sleep;
And in the dusk of dawn, dreaming like a great beast
Crouched low the hill. Suddenly, from the expectant east,
Forth from the womb of night flashed with a golden
                                    sweep
Dawn's scimitar of flame. Urgent with eager day
It clove the spire, and with the ten shades of delight,
Daubed with a dew-kissed brush the canvas of the
                                    night,
While to the waiting west the iris paled away.
Like drowsy swans the rose-downed clouds swam by,
And as I gazed, an influence still and unaware
Stole through my heart. The spire rose slenderly
                                    in prayer,
Crowned with the last faint star, and sceptred with
                                    the sky.

*SREDNI VASHTAR*

## WHOEVER LIVED FOR ENGLAND

Whoever lived for England – loved her well
And died with her green Aprils in their eyes,
Loved well this Hill, that like a sentinel
Keeps all this beauty under English skies –
Morning in June with first wild roses blowing
Full of the song of birds and leaf's unfolding,
Long days of broadening light and fields of sowing
And harvest time its golden riches holding –
Keeps all such ageless beauty multiplied
A hundred thousand times through all the long
Rich storied tapestry of England's pride,
To which this Hill and sacred tower belong;
Perchance a Crecy bowman saw the Hill
In darkening mind – and lay exceeding still.

W. A. G. KEMP
('Men like These' – 1947)

131

... now bows no more, but mimic battles claim
Our hero-spirits, and the martial din
Warns us of future, greater, fights to wage, and win.

(WALTER SYDNEY SICHEL)

## DAWN ATTACK

Breath hangs heavy on morning air
Trying to warm numb fingers;
Ferns waist-high about us –
We know the foe is there.
Dawn mists roll along the ground,
Shadows move to the sound
Of twigs snapping; nerves are taut
Caught to the pitch of war.


Figures show themselves, upright
Beyond the forests of ferns;
The enemy turns – we fire,
Long silences to shatter,
But still there's no reply.
Then from the mist there comes a cry –
A wail. We tense, nerves tight
As the wail grows stronger.
No longer hid, the bag-pipe player
Heralds himself in view;

As if on cue, they come,
Charging, firing, yelling their excitement.
The pipes! Reload - fire!
Gain courage! Reload - fire!
Till in triumphant waves
Through battered ferns
The battle's won.
We are dead, but still the bag-pipes play.

The enemy re-forms
But we, rebuked by lone bag-pipes,
Pick up our rifles, joke
And move away.
Black coffee and ginger pudding for breakfast -
Community Service is not for me!

GRAHAM HILL

(Sgt in C.C.F)

You go forth where your brothers went,
And the shadows gather round;
With last lights out, and the camp-fire's spent,
From the veldt dead voices sound,
Voices that ask "IS IT WELL WITH THE HILL,
Now as in the days that were?
Is it well?"
And phantom sentries still challenge you
"Who goes there —
You? —
Pass, Friend — All's well."

G. TOWNSEND WARNER

"Good night, Jonathan. I'm going to turn in; we shall be astir before daybreak. Over the veldt the stars are shining. It's so light, that I can just make out the hill upon which, I hope, our flag will be waving within a few hours. The sight of this hill brings back our Hill. If I shut my eyes, I can see it plainly, as we used to see it from the tower, with the Spire rising out of the heart of the old school. I have the absurd conviction strong in me that, tomorrow, I shall get up the hill here faster and easier than the other fellows because you and I have so often run up our Hill together ~ God bless it ~ and you! Goodnight."

HORACE ANNESLEY VACHELL.
(The Hill ~1905)

THE END

...then as the sun fell full upon the page
And pointed shadow cast,
I fancied that the spire,
Like some old story-teller,
Did trace its tale;
And I at one with fine-poised, fragile quill
Was but instrument to that Will.

THE CALLIGRAPHER

# INDEX